REVISE KEY STAGE 2 SATs
English

REVISION GUIDE

Expected Standard

Series Consultant: Janice Pimm

Author: Giles Clare

This revision guide is written for students who aim to perform at the expected national standard in English in their Year 6 SATs.

For students who hope to perform above the expected standard, check out:

Revise Key Stage 2 SATs English Revision Guide:
Above Expected Standard   9781292145990

Revise Key Stage 2 SATs English Revision Workbook:
Above Expected Standard   9781292145983

For the full range of Pearson revision titles visit:
www.pearsonschools.co.uk/revise

ALWAYS LEARNING   **PEARSON**

Contents

Grammar

1. Nouns
2. Noun phrases
3. Pronouns
4. Possessive pronouns
5. Determiners
6. Adjectives
7. Present tense
8. Past tense
9. Perfect & future tenses
10. Tense consistency
11. Modal verbs
12. Adverbs
13. Adverbial phrases
14. Conjunctions
15. Prepositions
16. Statements and questions
17. Commands and exclamations
18. Subject and object
19. Active and passive
20. Phrases
21. Main clauses
22. Subordinate clauses
23. Relative clauses
24. Subject–verb agreement
25. Standard English

Punctuation

26. Capital letters
27. Ending a sentence
28. Commas in lists
29. Commas for clarity
30. Parenthesis
31. Colons
32. Semi-colons
33. Apostrophes: possession
34. Apostrophes: contraction
35. Punctuating speech
36. Hyphens and single dashes

Spelling

37. Word families
38. Prefixes
39. Suffixes
40. Synonyms and antonyms
41. Plurals
42. Tricky spellings
43. More tricky spellings
44. Homophones

Writing

45 Audience and purpose
46 Planning and organising
47 Writing and editing
48 Checking
49 Writing articles
50 Writing explanations
51 Writing persuasive letters
52 Writing balanced arguments
53 Writing stories

Reading

54 Reading skills: close meaning
55 Reading skills: the whole text
56 Question types: selected answers
57 Question types: free answers
58–59 Non-fiction text
60 Non-fiction features
61 Retrieving and recording
62 Point, Evidence, Explain (PEE)
63 Summarising
64–65 Fiction text
66 Character
67 Theme
68 Finding meaning
69 Inference
70 Predicting
71 Making comparisons
72 Authors' language
73 Poem
74 Reading poetry
75 Similes and metaphors
76 Personification
77 Alliteration and onomatopoeia

78–82 Answers

A small bit of small print
The Standards and Testing Agency publishes Sample Test Materials on its website. This is the official content and this book should be used in conjunction with it. The questions in *Now try this* have been written to help you practise every topic in the book. Remember: the real test questions may not look like this.

Introduction

About your tests

At the end of Year 6, you will take tests to find out about your English skills. This book will help you revise all of the important skills you need for your tests.

- There will be one spelling test. Your teacher will read 20 words out loud. You need to write down the correct spellings. This test will take about 15 minutes.
- There will be one grammar test. This test will ask you questions about spelling, punctuation and grammar. You will have 45 minutes to do this test.
- There will be one reading test. You will have to read three texts and answer questions about them. You will have 1 hour to do this test.

Your teacher will look at some of your pieces of writing but there won't be a writing test.

Using this book

Each page of this book is about a different skill. Use the checkboxes at the top of the page to track your progress:

Had a look ☐ Tick this box when you've read the page.

Nearly there ☐ Tick this box when you understand the page quite well.

Nailed it! ☐ Tick this box when you understand the page really well.

Had a look ☐   Nearly there ☐   Nailed it! ☐   **Grammar**

Nouns

A **noun** is a naming word for a person, place, thing or idea. A noun can be **singular** (one) or **plural** (more than one).

Common nouns

Common nouns refer to people or things in general. Some nouns, called **abstract nouns**, name ideas or feelings that you can't see or touch. Other nouns, called **collective nouns**, name groups of things.

singular common noun → *collective noun* ↙

The <u>fox</u> saw the <u>brood</u> of <u>chickens</u>. It couldn't resist the <u>temptation</u>.

↗ *abstract noun*   *plural common noun* ↖

A common noun only needs a capital letter at the start of a sentence.

Proper nouns

A **proper noun** names a particular person, place or thing. It always begins with a capital letter.

days and months ↘   *names of people* ↓ ↓

In <u>September</u>, when <u>Sarah</u> and <u>Kamal</u> went to <u>Paris</u> in <u>France</u>, they visited the <u>Eiffel</u> <u>Tower</u>.

↖ *particular places*

Proper nouns are also used for special times such as **Christmas**, companies such as **Pearson** and titles such as *Alice in Wonderland*.

Example

Underline all the words in this sentence that should start with a capital letter.

<u>last</u> <u>tuesday</u> in <u>london</u>, <u>ricky</u> <u>edwards</u> walked by the <u>river</u> <u>thames</u> on his way to <u>trafalgar</u> <u>square</u>.

Some proper nouns are made up of more than one word, which should both have capitals, like the River Thames or Trafalgar Square.

Now try this

1. Which of the words below are nouns? Which type of nouns are they?

   happiness   rabbits   happy   herd   slowly   Ben
   jumped   Easter   they   victory deckchair

1

Grammar

Had a look ☐   Nearly there ☐   Nailed it! ☐

Noun phrases

You can use **noun phrases** to add extra information to nouns to give more detail and be more clear.

Noun phrases

A noun phrase is a group of words that work together like a noun. The noun is the main word in the phrase.

The woman filled up her car with some petrol.

The, her and some tell us more clearly about each noun.

Each underlined phrase is a simple noun phrase.

Expanded noun phrases

You can expand noun phrases to add more precise or interesting details.

Each underlined phrase is an expanded noun phrase.

The giant, pink jellyfish stung the inexperienced scuba diver on his right leg.

The simplest way to expand a noun phrase is to add adjectives.

All of the other words add detail to the noun 'news'.

The news about that missing diver is very worrying.

Example

Identify each noun first and then look for any other words that tell you about those nouns.

Underline the three noun phrases in this sentence.

People over 70 should see their doctor about a winter flu injection.

Now try this

See page 6 for more about adjectives.

1. Think of five nouns and add a word to each to make five simple noun phrases.
2. Add an adjective to each of the noun phrases below.

   the girl   his toy   some paper   your fish   that house

3. Rewrite the sentence below and expand the noun phrases to make the mood more frightening. Remember to use the correct punctuation in your answer.

   The boy wandered into the room.

Had a look ☐   Nearly there ☐   Nailed it! ☐   **Grammar**

Pronouns

Pronouns can replace nouns and noun phrases, show ownership or refer back to nouns.

Personal pronouns

You can use pronouns instead of nouns to talk about people or things. These two sentences sound clumsy and repetitive together.

> Emily found a ten-pound note. Emily put the ten-pound note in a box.

proper noun   noun phrase   noun

This is less repetitive and reflects how you might say it out loud.

> Emily found a ten-pound note. She put it in a box.

pronoun replaces proper noun   pronoun replaces noun phrase

Choosing the right personal pronoun

You must use the correct personal pronoun depending on whom or what you are referring to.

Examples of personal pronouns include **I, me, he, him, her, we, us, they** and **them**.

Example

Underline all the pronouns in the phrase below.

Mum asked <u>me</u> if <u>I</u> had reminded Evie about the present. <u>I</u> said <u>she</u> had already left with Dad to buy <u>it</u>.

> Look for the words that replace someone's name or a common noun.

Now try this

1. Underline all the **pronouns** in the following sentences.

   We saw them at the cinema. They told me about the film. It wasn't very good apparently so we decided that it would have been a waste of time for us to see it.

Grammar — Had a look ☐ Nearly there ☐ Nailed it! ☐

Possessive pronouns

Possessive pronouns are used to show who or what **owns** something.

Used with nouns

You can use a possessive pronoun with a noun or noun phrase.

used with nouns	my	your	his/her/its	our	their
replacing nouns	mine	yours	his/hers/its	ours	theirs

tells you who the first cat belongs to (them) → Their cat is much thinner than our cat, but its appetite is huge.

tells you who the other cat belongs to (us)

refers to the first cat's appetite

Possessive pronouns sometimes end in **s** but never need an apostrophe.

it's is a contraction not a pronoun; **it's** always means **it is**.

Replacing nouns

You can also use possessive pronouns to replace nouns or noun phrases.

Leave Alice's bag alone. That bag is hers. It is not yours!

Using 'hers' and 'yours' means you don't have to say 'her bag' and 'your bag'.

Example

Complete the sentence below with two suitable possessive pronouns.

My friend said that the pencil was his.

Another answer might be Your friend said that the pencil was hers.

Now try this

1. Replace the noun phrases in this sentence with possessive pronouns.
   Those books are my books although that magazine is your magazine.
2. How would you correct the punctuation in the sentence below?
   Although its nearly six o'clock, its still not time for the cat to have it's tea.

Had a look ☐   Nearly there ☐   Nailed it! ☐   **Grammar**

Determiners

A **determiner** is a word that comes before a noun to make the noun specific or general. A determiner comes at the beginning of a noun phrase.

Articles

The most common type of determiner is the **article**. You can use **a** before a consonant or **an** before a vowel for things in general. Use **the** for specific things.

refers to one specific astronaut → *refers to the specific spaceship he was in* → *just any asteroid, not a specific one* →

The young astronaut lost control of the spaceship and landed on an asteroid.

Types of determiner

determiners	a, an, the	this, that, those, these	numbers, some, any, every, another, other, no, a lot of, all	my, your, his, her, its, our, their
what they are used for	to begin noun phrases	to make a noun more specific	to show amounts	to show who things belong to
example	An elderly man sat on a bench in the park.	That teacher marked all those books.	Every day, some people forget to eat five portions of fruit and vegetables.	Our house is next to your garage.

Example

Identify all the noun phrases. The determiners come at the start of each one.

Circle all the determiners in the sentence below.

(This) morning, I ate (some) cereal and (two) pieces of toast for (my) breakfast.

Now try this

See page 2 for more about noun phrases.

1. Correct the **determiners** in the sentence below.
   A owl uses our face to gather sounds, just like an satellite dish collects signals for his television.

Grammar | Had a look ☐ | Nearly there ☐ | Nailed it! ☐

Adjectives

An **adjective** is a word that describes a noun.

Adjectives add detail

Adjectives can come before or after the nouns they describe.

These adjectives come before the noun (fish).

These adjectives come after the noun but still describe it.

The <u>small</u>, <u>beautiful</u> fish was <u>yellow</u> and <u>blue</u>.

You can use adjectives to make your descriptions more interesting and imaginative.

Read the text again but miss out the adjectives to see the difference they can make.

> The **exhausted**, **shivering** walker finally reached the **barren** peak of the **gloomy** hill. For a few moments, he took in the **wide**, **desolate** view. He frowned. **Dark**, **threatening** clouds were rolling up the **narrow** valley. A **sudden**, **violent** storm was approaching.

Comparative adjectives compare nouns

Adjectives ending in **-er** compare two nouns.
Adjectives ending in **-est** compare more than two nouns.

*For adjectives with three or more syllables, you use **more** and **most**, as in more/most important (im-por-tant)*

-er compares Harry and Aisha.

-est compares Jerome to everyone else.

Harry is <u>quicker</u> than Aisha but Jerome is the <u>fastest</u> runner.

Now try this

1. Find all the **adjectives** in the sentence below.
   The delicious, pink cake was sticky.
2. Complete the sentence below using the correct **comparative adjectives**.
   Aaron's mobile is <u>(good)</u> than mine, although Blake's is the <u>(thin)</u>.

Had a look ☐   Nearly there ☐   Nailed it! ☐   **Grammar**

Present tense

Verbs are often called 'doing' words, for example 'jump', 'eat' or 'shout'. Sometimes they are also 'being' words, for example 'am' or 'have'.
The **tense** of a verb tells you when it's happening.

Simple present

You use the **present tense** when you are talking about something that is happening in the present. In other words, now.

present tense of the verb 'to play' →
present tense of the verb 'to have' →
present tense of the verb 'to be' →

Jonny <u>plays</u> computer games. He <u>has</u> all the latest games. He <u>is</u> lucky.

Events in progress

You can use the present tense to talk about events that are still going on at the moment of speaking. This is known as the **present progressive**.

Two separate words make up this verb form. →
Use 'to be' and add the suffix 'ing' to the verb. →

Max <u>is swimming</u> as fast as he can but I <u>am floating</u> in the shallow end.

Example

Underline the verb form that is in the present progressive in the sentence below.

This form of the present tense has two parts. Look for verbs ending in 'ing'.

Although she tries her best, Suzie <u>is finding</u> her spellings difficult.

Now try this

1. Identify all the present tense verbs in the sentence below.
   I listen to music every day; in fact, my radio is playing right now.
2. How would you rewrite the verbs below in the present progressive tense?
   she runs   he studies hard   we ride our bikes   they are rude
3. Think of three sentences describing your morning routine in the present tense only.

Grammar — Had a look ☐ Nearly there ☐ Nailed it! ☐

Past tense

Like the present tense, verbs in the **past tense** can be written in two different ways.

Simple past

A verb in the **past tense** is used to show that an event has already happened in the past. It is usually made by adding the ending **–ed** to the verb.

past tense of the verb 'to sprint'   *past tense of the verb 'to jump'*

> Rosie <u>sprinted</u> along the track, <u>jumped</u> over the hurdles and <u>won</u> the race.

Some verbs don't end in **–ed**. We say 'won' not 'winned'.

past tense of the verb 'to win'

Past progressive

You can use the **past progressive** to talk about events that lasted for some time in the past.

Use 'to be' in the past tense.   *Add the suffix '–ing' to the verb.*

> The birds <u>were</u> <u>singing</u> in the trees all morning whilst I <u>was</u> <u>cooking</u> our special lunch.

Example

Which sentence in this passage uses the past progressive?

I entered the kitchen. <u>The kettle was boiling</u>. I turned it off.

Look for the key words 'was' and 'were' next to verbs ending in '–ing'.

Now try this

1. Find all the past tense verbs in the passage below.

   My parents were talking when someone knocked on the door. My dad looked puzzled. 'I wasn't expecting anyone,' he said.

2. How would you rewrite the verbs below in the simple past tense?

   it was raining   they were dancing   you were sulking   she was hurrying

3. Which are the most appropriate verb forms in the sentence below?

   While I *spoke/was speaking* to George, the door suddenly *slammed/was slamming*.

Had a look ☐   Nearly there ☐   Nailed it! ☐   Grammar

Perfect & future tenses

Perfect tense

The **perfect tense** is used to show that an event happened in the past but not at a specific time. It is made by putting **have**, **has** or **had** before a verb.

'has' + past tense   'have' + past tense

This verb form is called the **present perfect (has / have)**.

Grandma <u>has bought</u> me a DVD for my birthday but I <u>have seen</u> it already.

'had' + past tense

This verb form is called the **past perfect (had)**.

Harry <u>had visited</u> Spain several times, but Florence <u>had</u> never <u>been</u> there.

'had' + past tense

Future tense

You can write about events in the future in a number of ways.

Sara <u>is going to arrive</u> tomorrow.
Her plane <u>lands</u> at seven.
We <u>will drive</u> to the airport at six.

Use '**be going to**' with a verb.
Use the **present tense** even though it's a future event (tomorrow at seven).
Use '**will**' followed by a verb.

Example

Which of the verbs below are in the present perfect tense?

(I have said)   you had eaten   (she has left)

Now try this

1. Which of the verbs below are in the past perfect tense?
   we have finished   it had happened   they have arrived
2. How would you rewrite the sentence below in the future tense?
   I leave for school after breakfast and I return at four.

9

Grammar

Had a look ☐   Nearly there ☐   Nailed it! ☐

Tense consistency

Different tenses use different verb forms. In general, make sure you use **the same tense** throughout a sentence or clause.

What is the time frame?

If the action happens in the same time frame, the tense should stay the same. Look what happens when you change tenses but the time frame is the same.

past tense → *present tense* → *past tense*

> Mike jumped out of bed, puts on his slippers and went downstairs.

The correct sentence should say: *all verbs in the past tense to make it consistent*

> Mike jumped out of bed, put on his slippers and went downstairs.

Further examples

Compare the sentences on the left, which include mistakes, with those on the right, which are the correct versions. You will see that the tenses only change if the time frame changes.

Yesterday I swim in the pool and then ran home.	Yesterday I swam in the pool and then ran home.
He should go to the doctor, buy some medicine and went to bed.	He should go to the doctor, buy some medicine and go to bed.
They are enjoying the bread that I bake this morning.	They are enjoying the bread that I baked this morning.
The first visitors arrived as soon as the new park will open.	The first visitors arrived as soon as the new park had opened.

Now try this

1. Correct the **tenses** in the passage below.

   Earlier this morning, Sammy went to the zoo, where he sees a mysterious animal. He should not have go closer, but he couldn't resist. The animal, which has pink spots and blue toenails, snarls and snorted at him. The smell will be terrible.

Had a look ☐   Nearly there ☐   Nailed it! ☐

Grammar

Modal verbs

A **modal verb**, such as 'may', 'can' or 'must', comes before another verb to change its meaning.

Modal verbs show possibility

You can use a modal verb to show how possible, certain or necessary something is.

how possible something is

It's so cold it <u>may</u> snow tonight but it <u>might</u> melt by the morning.

how certain something is

They <u>should</u> be here by now. I <u>can</u> guess what's happened; they <u>will</u> be stuck in traffic.

> Common modal verbs include will, would, can, could, may, might, shall, should, ought to and must.

how necessary something is

We <u>ought to</u> leave. We <u>mustn't</u> be late for the wedding.

Example

> The modal verbs always come before the main verbs, even in questions.

Underline the modal verbs in the passage below.

<u>Can</u> Holly really speak three languages? And <u>would</u> Pedro like to learn four?

Now try this

1. Find the modal verb in the sentence below.
   My favourite football team could win the league cup if they win their next match.
2. Which modal verbs are missing from the sentences below?
   _____ you read when you were four?
   I _____ find my glasses anywhere.
   Suki _____ play the piano perfectly.
   George didn't get off the bus; he _____ have missed it.

Grammar — Had a look ☐   Nearly there ☐   Nailed it! ☐

Adverbs

An **adverb** is a describing word that tells you more about a **verb**. Many adverbs end in –ly. Adverbs can also describe other **word classes** and **clauses**.

Describing verbs

You can use an adverb to describe when, how or where something is happening.

Rosie <u>immediately</u> started running <u>fast</u> and rushed <u>outside</u>.

> Some adverbs don't end in –ly.

- describes the verb 'started' (when)
- describes the verb 'running' (how)
- describes the verb 'rushed' (where)

Other uses

You can also use adverbs to describe **adjectives**, other **adverbs** and even whole **clauses**.

Match Report

Beech Tree Primary ...... **3** Rose Bush Juniors **2**

Yesterday's match was <u>really</u> **exciting**. With the match tied, Aaron set off in the final minute and dribbled <u>very</u> **skillfully** up the pitch and shot from miles out. <u>Eventually, the ball hit the back of the net.</u> Beech Tree won!

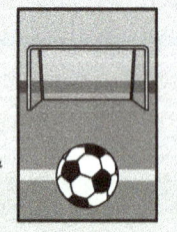

- The adverb <u>really</u> describes the adjective **exciting**.
- The adverb <u>very</u> describes the adverb **skillfully**.
- The adverb <u>eventually</u> describes **the whole clause** that follows.

> Adverbs are often found before or after the verb they describe. They can also be found at the beginning of a sentence.

Example

Underline the adverbs in the sentence below.

Reuben climbed <u>slowly</u> into bed and was <u>soon</u> dreaming.

Now try this

> See pages 23–25 for more about clauses.

1. Add two adverbs to the sentence below.

   'Let me out,' shouted Jack.

2. Circle all the adverbs in the passage below.

   Fortunately, it wasn't raining hard when we finally got to the beach. Instead, it was beautifully sunny!

Had a look ☐   Nearly there ☐   Nailed it! ☐   **Grammar**

Adverbial phrases

An **adverbial phrase** is a group of words that acts as an adverb. It can tell you **how**, **where** and **when** something is happening.

Describing the verb

Adverbial phrases give more detail about verbs.

I have a special power. I can see <u>far into the future</u>! A strange creature will arrive <u>by teleportation</u>. It will appear <u>one hundred years from now</u>.

The adverbial <u>far into the future</u> describes **where**.

The adverbial <u>by teleportation</u> describes **how**.

The adverbial <u>one hundred years from now</u> describes **when**.

Fronted adverbials

You can also put an adverbial phrase at the start (front) of a sentence.

<u>After the party</u>, Sophie went straight to bed.

Don't forget to put a comma after the fronted adverbial.

This fronted adverbial describes when Sophie went to bed.

Example

Identify the verb (disappeared) and find the group of words that describe how, where or when it's happening.

Circle the adverbial phrase in the sentence below.

Our old friends, Zoe and Jack, disappeared (early this morning before breakfast).

Now try this

1. Find all the adverbial phrases in the sentence below.
   Once upon a time, an old man lived very happily in a dark cave, where he made clothes all by himself.
2. Rewrite this sentence so that it begins with a fronted adverbial.
   Logan knocked on the ancient door of the old house.
3. Think of a sentence with an adverbial phrase that describes where something is happening.

13

Conjunctions

You use **conjunctions** to link words, phrases or clauses together.

Co-ordinating conjunctions

Conjunctions such as 'and', 'but' and 'or' co-ordinate (link) words, phrases or clauses of equal importance.

> Nadia's favourite clothes are blue socks <u>and</u> purple shoes.

links the two noun phrases of equal importance: 'blue socks' and 'purple shoes'

> Clauses contain verbs (was/wasn't).

> Hamish was hungry <u>but</u> there wasn't any food.

first clause   links two clauses of equal importance   second clause

Subordinating conjunctions

Some conjunctions such as 'because', 'while' and 'although' introduce a **subordinate clause**.

> Dewi reads a book on the sofa <u>whenever it is raining</u>.

main clause   subordinating conjunction   subordinate clause

A subordinate clause does not make sense as a sentence on its own. It only makes sense when used with a **main clause**.

There are two subordinate clauses in the same sentence. The main clause is 'Freya enjoyed winter sports'.

Example

Underline all the conjunctions in the sentence below.

Freya enjoyed winter sports <u>until</u> she broke her leg <u>whilst</u> she was skiing.

Now try this

See pages 21–22 for more about main and subordinate clauses.

1. Rewrite the sentence below with appropriate conjunctions.

_____ it was snowing, Howard _____ Tamwar played football _____ they lost their ball.

Had a look ☐   Nearly there ☐   Nailed it! ☐   **Grammar**

Prepositions

A **preposition** is a word that shows where something is or when something is happening. It comes before a noun or pronoun. A preposition can also show the direction of travel.

Prepositions to show position or direction

Some examples include **above**, **under**, **beneath**, **inside**, **between**, **by**, **near**, **against**, **through**, **to**, **past**, **across**, **along**, **over**, **off** and **up**.

> The tired teacher sat <u>behind</u> the desk with his feet <u>on</u> the tabletop.

shows where the teacher is in relation to the desk

shows where his feet are in relation to the tabletop

> The teacher stood up slowly, edged <u>around</u> the desk and walked <u>towards</u> the door.

shows the teacher's direction of travel in relation to the door

shows his direction of travel in relation to the desk

Prepositions to show time

Other prepositions show when things are happening.

> <u>On</u> Monday, we are going swimming <u>after</u> school <u>until</u> six o'clock.

Example

Underline the prepositions in the sentence below.

<u>Since</u> last week, I have done my homework <u>in</u> the kitchen before I eat dinner.

'Before' is not used as a preposition here because it introduces a subordinate clause (I eat dinner) not a noun.

Now try this

See page 22 for more about subordinate clauses and conjunctions.

1. Correct the prepositions in the sentence below.
   Katy walked since two hours under the dark tunnel. Finally, she saw a light coming around her.

Grammar   Had a look ☐   Nearly there ☐   Nailed it! ☐

Statements and questions

A sentence is a group of words that must contain a **subject** and a **verb**. It expresses a complete thought. A sentence can have one or more **clauses**. There are four main types of sentence.

Statements

A statement states a fact and ends with a full stop.

> The giraffe is the tallest land mammal.

subject   verb   full stop

Questions

A question asks something and always ends with a question mark. You can form a question by starting with a question word, by using an inversion or by adding a question tag.

question	what you need
What is your favourite colour?	a question word
Are you coming for tea?	subject and verb swap places (you ↔ are)
Lydia is very late, isn't she?	a question tag

Example

Punctuate these sentences correctly.

Those are my chocolates you're eating, aren't they?
How could you? The box is nearly empty.

Look for capital letters to see where punctuation might be missing.

Now try this

See page 18 for more about subjects and objects.

1. Change this question to a statement.
   Is Mason fit enough to play in the match today?
2. Change this statement to a question.
   Katrina and Scott are the winners of the science competition.

Had a look ☐   Nearly there ☐   Nailed it! ☐   **Grammar**

Commands and exclamations

Commands

A **command** tells someone to do something. It might be an instruction or an order. A command always contains a 'bossy' verb called an **imperative**.

If a bear attacks you, <u>punch</u> it on the snout.

This instruction ends in a full stop.

'bossy' (imperative) verbs

<u>Stop</u> right there! Do not <u>open</u> that box!

These orders end in exclamation marks for emphasis.

Exclamations

An **exclamation** shows strong feelings such as surprise, joy or fear. This sentence type can start with **What** or **How** and will include a verb.

<u>What</u> an amazing show that was!
<u>How</u> brilliant the dancers were!

Other phrases can end with an exclamation mark but these are not called exclamations in the test.

An exclamation always ends in an exclamation mark.

Example

Underline the command in the sentences below.

"The second half is starting," called out Bailey.
"<u>Hurry up</u>. What a match this is!"

A command often starts with a 'bossy' verb and doesn't always end in an exclamation mark.

Now try this

1. Which of these sentences are exclamations and which are commands?
   Go up to your room!
   What a lovely day it is!
   Push the buzzer and enter.
   How shocking that was!

17

Grammar

Had a look ☐ Nearly there ☐ Nailed it! ☐

Subject and object

All clauses and sentences must have a **subject** and a verb. Many also contain an **object**.

Subject

The subject is the **main focus** of a sentence. It's who or what the sentence is about. The subject can be a noun, a pronoun or a noun phrase.

subject (proper noun)   subject (pronoun)

Annabelle is nine. She likes scooters.
Her favourite scooter has red stripes.

subject (noun phrase)

The subject is often the first thing mentioned in a sentence.

Object

The **object** in a sentence is the thing that the verb is being **done to** or **done with**.

Ravi loves cakes. Dougie likes them too. Paige eats sticky buns.

object (noun)   object (pronoun)   object (noun phrase)

Example

The subject and object come either side of the verb (gave).

Underline and label the **subject (S)** and the **object (O)** in the sentence below.

She (S) gave the priceless coin (O) to me.

Now try this

See page 24 for more about subject-verb agreement.

1. Is the underlined text in each sentence a subject or an object?

   Candace was singing <u>a song</u>.
   The cat swallowed <u>it</u>.
   <u>The desperate prisoner</u> disappeared into the forest.
   <u>We</u> were dancing, weren't we?

Had a look ☐ Nearly there ☐ Nailed it! ☐   **Grammar**

Active and passive

You can write a sentence or a clause in the **active** or **passive voice**.

Active voice

You use the active voice when the **subject** of the sentence is the thing 'doing' the verb.

The tiger hunted the deer.
subject   verb   object

The subject (the tiger) is 'doing' the hunting; this is the active voice.

Passive voice

You use the passive voice when the **subject** has the verb 'done' to it. A passive sentence often has the word **by** after the verb.

The deer was hunted by the tiger.
subject   verb   object

The object has become the subject; the action is being 'done' to it.

Example

Rewrite the sentence below in the passive voice.
The howling wind blew Ronan off his feet.

Ronan was blown off his feet by the howling wind.

*The object (Ronan) must become the subject. The verb form in the passive is formed from **to be** and the past tense.*

Now try this

See page 18 for more about subjects and objects.

1. Is the sentence below written in the active or passive voice?
   By law, tigers are now protected.
2. Rewrite the passage below so that it is written in the active voice.
   Remember to punctuate your answer correctly.

   The alarm was tripped by the thief. The police were alerted by the security guard but, before they arrived, the thief was grabbed by two passers-by.

19

Grammar

Had a look ☐ Nearly there ☐ Nailed it! ☐

Phrases

A **phrase** is a group of words that means something on its own but does not make a clause or sentence.

What's in a phrase?

In a phrase, you might have a noun, adjective, adverb, preposition or conjunction or a combination of these things. However, a phrase does **not** include a verb.

noun phrase → The wind plucked the leaves one by one from the tree.
← adverb phrase
↑ preposition phrase

Remember, none of these phrases make a sentence on their own.

expanded noun phrase (adjectives and noun) → The lazy, overweight lion was sleeping happily until the cubs woke it up.
← conjunction phrase

Notice that the verbs are not part of these phrases.

Example

Underline the preposition phrase in this sentence.

Arisha hid the packet of sweets <u>under her bed</u> with great care.

*The preposition **under** is followed by the noun phrase **her bed**. With great care shows how she hid the sweets; it's an adverb phrase.*

Now try this

See page 2 for more about noun phrases.

1. Look at the underlined words in the sentence. Are they used as an expanded noun phrase, a preposition phrase, a conjunction phrase or an adverb phrase?

   <u>The strawberry-flavour frozen yoghurt</u> is the best.

20

Had a look ☐   Nearly there ☐   Nailed it! ☐   **Grammar**

Main clauses

A **clause** must contain a subject and a verb. Some clauses are joined or introduced by conjunctions.

A **main clause** makes sense on its own as a sentence.

subject → The clouds *← verb* burst. We *← subject* sheltered *← verb* under a tree.

Joining main clauses

Sometimes you have two main clauses of **equal importance** in a sentence.
You can use **co-ordinating conjunctions** such as 'and', 'but' and 'or' to join them.

first main clause → My mum hates singing competitions on television **yet** she loves karaoke.

co-ordinating conjunction   *second main clause*

> These two clauses are equally important.

> Don't join two main clauses with a comma. This is called comma splicing. You need a conjunction.

Example

> 'We' is the subject and 'sneaked' is the verb.

Underline the main clause in this sentence.

At six o'clock yesterday, before dawn, <u>we sneaked silently out of the house</u>.

Now try this

> See page 14 for more about conjunctions.

1. Join this sentence with an appropriate co-ordinating conjunction.
   Shani's pony doesn't like carrots _____ will it eat parsnips.
2. Which are the two main clauses in this sentence?
   Following his accident, Jarrod spent two days in hospital but, against the advice of his doctor, he went home early.

21

Grammar

Had a look ☐   Nearly there ☐   Nailed it! ☐

Subordinate clauses

A **subordinate clause** is introduced by a subordinating conjunction. It does not make sense as a sentence on its own.

main clause → *subordinating conjunction* ↓

> We sheltered under a large umbrella **while** it was pouring with rain.

↑ *subordinate clause*

> The subordinate clause only makes sense when it's attached to the main clause.

Positioning subordinate clauses

In most cases, you can put a subordinate clause before or after the main clause.

main clause →

> The climber carried on towards the summit although his oxygen supply had run out.
>
> Although his oxygen supply had run out, the climber carried on towards the summit.

↑ *subordinate clause*

> When you put the subordinate clause before the main clause, use a comma to separate them.

Example

Underline the subordinate clause in this sentence.

<u>When Nick shouted at the ducks</u>, his mum told him off.

> The subordinate clause does not make sense on its own.

Now try this

> See page 14 for more about conjunctions.

1. Which are the subordinating conjunctions in this sentence?
   Unless it was a special occasion, my grandparents always went to bed early because they were getting old.

2. Rewrite this sentence to put the subordinate clause before the main clause. Remember to punctuate your answer correctly.
   You must bring your toys inside before you have your tea.

Had a look ☐   Nearly there ☐   Nailed it! ☐   **Grammar**

Relative clauses

A **relative clause** adds detail to a noun. It always comes after the noun it is describing. It is a type of subordinate clause.

A relative clause begins with a relative pronoun: **who**, **whose**, **that** or **which**.

Who and whose

You use **who** and **whose** when you are talking about people.

> You use commas to separate relative clauses from main clauses.

noun — relative pronoun — relative clause

My uncle, who lives in the United States, is coming to visit.
The girl, whose friends had run away, was angry and upset.

noun — relative pronoun — relative clause

Which and that

You use **that** and **which** when you are talking about things.

noun — relative pronoun — relative clause

The apple, which was old and soft, tasted horrible.
The plane that was due to land this morning has been delayed.

noun — relative pronoun — relative clause

> Don't use a comma before that.

> A relative clause always starts with **who**, **whose**, **which** or **that**.

Example

Circle the relative clause in this sentence.

Donald, (whose hands were enormous), was a great goalkeeper.

> See pages 3–4 for more about pronouns.

Now try this

1. Which is the correct relative pronoun to complete the sentence below?

   whose   who   that   which

   The ice-creams, _____ had been sitting in the sunshine, had melted.

2. Which is the relative clause in the sentence below?

   My grandad, who is 72, is running the marathon.

23

Grammar Had a look ☐   Nearly there ☐   Nailed it! ☐

Subject–verb agreement

When you write a clause or sentence, you must make sure that the verb 'agrees' with the subject.

Is the subject singular or plural?

The verb form you choose depends on whether the subject is **singular** (one) or **plural** (more than one).

singular subject — singular verb form

The girl **plays** tag rugby.
The girls **play** tag rugby.

plural subject — plural verb form

Notice how the spelling of the verb changes.

Most verbs have two forms in the present tense.

I, we, you or they...	he, she or it...
play	plays
do	does
have	has
rush	rushes
are (except I am)	is

Example

Circle the correct verbs in the sentences below to make the subjects and verbs agree.

Read the sentence back to yourself to see if it sounds right.

(Isn't) / aren't it hot outside today? I wishes /(wish) I have / (had) a cold drink.

Now try this

See page 7 for more about present-tense verbs.

1. Change each <u>verb</u> in the sentences below so that it agrees with the subject.
   Bertie <u>sing</u> really well.
   Kayley and Jared <u>brushes</u> the kitchen floor.
2. Change each <u>subject</u> in the sentences below so that it agrees with the verb.
   The <u>pilot</u> fly their planes.
   The <u>trains</u> is late.
   The <u>kettle</u> have boiled.

Had a look ☐   Nearly there ☐   Nailed it! ☐   **Grammar**

Standard English

In your writing, you should use **Standard English**. This means using grammatically correct language that avoids slang and dialect words.

What you say and what you write

Many people use **non-Standard English** in everyday conversation. You should avoid using it in writing. Here are some common examples.

Non-Standard English (spoken)	Standard English (written)
We was at school.	We were at school.
Me and Ben watched the football.	Ben and I watched the football.
I can't hear nothing.	I can't hear anything.
You should of thought of that.	You should have thought of that.

Slang and dialect

Slang is casual language that is not Standard English. A **dialect** is a way of speaking used in a particular area. Neither should be used in writing unless you want to create a casual, chatty effect, for example, in direct speech.

> You can still use some contractions (I've/haven't) in Standard English.

"I'm off to the <u>chippy</u> for some <u>scran</u>. You want <u>owt</u>?" asked Dom.

slang word for a fish and chip shop

dialect words for 'food' and 'anything'

See page 51 for more about formal and informal language.

Example

Correct the underlined verb and determiner in this sentence, using Standard English.
We <u>was</u> just going out to watch <u>them</u> fireworks.

We <u>were</u> just going out to watch <u>those</u> fireworks.

> Make sure the subject and verb agree. **These** and **those** are the plural forms of **this** and **that**.

Now try this

1. Rewrite the sentences below using Standard English.

   Me dad wants to go cinema but I don't wanna go.
   We ain't done nothin' wrong.

25

Capital letters

You use **capital letters** to start a sentence, for proper nouns and for the personal pronoun I.

At the start of a sentence

All sentences begin with a capital letter.

← capital letter   ← capital letter

My friend saw the new movie. He said it was brilliant!

The full stop marks the end of the first sentence.

Proper nouns

Proper nouns always begin with a capital letter.

*Unless they start the sentence, common nouns do **not** need capital letters.*

← days and months

On Tuesday, while Mrs Brown was on holiday in Wales, a thief stole her car.

← names of people and places

Other types of proper nouns include special times such as Diwali, titles such as Treasure Island and languages such as French.

A person's title (Mr) and name (Ashton Adams) need capital letters.

Example

In the sentence below, underline all the words that should start with a **capital letter**.

in january 1956, mr ashton adams performed on a unicycle at the circus in berlin.

See page 1 for more about common and proper nouns.

Now try this

1. Which of the words in the sentences below should start with a **capital letter**?

   it's time i went to birmingham.
   kathy borrowed that money last march. now it's nearly november!
   the st luke's church choir sang carols in italian and german at christmas.

Had a look ☐   Nearly there ☐   Nailed it! ☐   **Punctuation**

Ending a sentence

There are three main ways you can end a sentence: with a **full stop**, a **question mark** or an **exclamation mark**.

Full stop

Most sentences are statements that end in a full stop. Remember, a sentence contains a clause (subject and verb) or a number of linked clauses.

capital letter   *first clause*   *second clause*

We sent Keira a present because it was her birthday.   *full stop*

Question marks and exclamation marks

Questions always end in a question mark.

What is the time? Are we nearly there? It's not too late, is it?

questions

Exclamation marks are always used to end an exclamation. They are sometimes also used to make a command or statement more forceful or important.

> You use a question mark or exclamation mark instead of a full stop. Never use both.

command

Get down off the roof right now! What a silly boy you are! That is so dangerous!

exclamation   *statement*

Example

> See page 51 for more about formal and informal language.

Insert the correct punctuation marks into the sentences below.

You forgot to feed the cat, didn't you? Tiddles must be absolutely starving!

> The second sentence could also end with a full stop instead.

Now try this

1. What punctuation is missing from the passage below?

    Was it time to go home The chef looked at his watch It was eleven o'clock He smiled Finally, his shift was over What a day

Punctuation

Had a look ☐   Nearly there ☐   Nailed it! ☐

Commas in lists

Commas have lots of uses. You use them to make your writing clearer and to avoid confusion.

Commas to separate items

In a list, you must put commas between the items to separate them.

list of nouns →

Mina ordered a new dress, blue shoes, a handbag and a scarf.

Use 'and' or 'or' before the final item instead of a comma.

list of verbs ↓   *list of adjectives* ↓

Belle loved to <u>act</u>, <u>sing</u> and <u>dance</u>. She was <u>talented</u>, <u>ambitious</u> and <u>fun</u>.

Well-known phrases

Some pairs of nouns are well-known phrases that shouldn't be separated. Look at how you use commas to separate items in this case.

Lucas loved burgers, nuggets, <u>doughnuts and fish and chips</u>.   ← 'fish and chips' counts as one item

Example

The phrase 'black and blue' counts as one item. It means bruised.

Add the commas in the correct places in the sentence below.
After rugby, Karl was exhausted muddy sore and black and blue.

After rugby, Karl was exhausted, muddy, sore and black and blue.

Now try this

1. Circle the correct comma in the sentence below.
   Would you like strawberries, yoghurt, or a piece, of watermelon?
2. Where should the commas be placed in this list?
   Mohan had three books two pens a hat and a sandwich in his bag.
3. Think of three more noun phrases (like 'fish and chips') that are often heard together.

Had a look ☐   Nearly there ☐   Nailed it! ☐   **Punctuation**

Commas for clarity

Commas can be used to separate different parts of a sentence to make the meaning clear.

Commas to separate clauses

See page 22 for more about subordinate clauses.

You often use commas to separate **subordinate clauses** and **fronted adverbials** from **main clauses**.

Early that morning, Agnes went ice-skating.

Always put a comma after a fronted adverbial.

The scientist, who was very curious, discovered a new element.

You can put commas around a subordinate clause that provides extra information.

We went indoors because it was freezing.

Don't put commas around a subordinate clause if it's important to the meaning of the sentence.

Example

Use commas to punctuate this sentence correctly.

Despite the rain, Cloud, who was the most powerful stallion, galloped on.

The commas are used to make the meaning much clearer.

Now try this

1. Which are the correct commas in the sentence below?
   Before, dawn, Leila, whose kitten, was sick, took it, straight to the vets.
2. Insert two commas to make the meaning of the sentence below clearer.
   Some kangaroos which can grow up to two metres tall are extremely strong.

29

Punctuation | Had a look ☐ | Nearly there ☐ | Nailed it! ☐

Parenthesis

A **parenthesis** is extra information inserted into a sentence. It is shown by using **commas**, **brackets** or **dashes**. If you take the parenthesis away, the sentence will still make sense.

Commas

You can insert a relative clause between two commas with or without using a relative pronoun.

> Stuart MacKenzie, <u>a horse trainer from Stirling</u>, received a letter from the Queen.

Notice that 'who was' has been dropped from the relative clause.

extra information between the commas

Brackets and dashes

You can put a pair of brackets or a pair of dashes around extra information in the middle or at the end of a sentence.

Notice that the first word in the brackets doesn't need a capital letter.

> Our holiday to Spain was a disaster (<u>the hotel was a building site</u>).

The brackets separate this information.

> Admiring the sea of stars overhead – <u>it was a crisp, clear night</u> – Wai Lin felt full of wonder.

Dashes are longer than hyphens.

Remember, the sentence must always make sense without the parenthesis.

Example

Insert a pair of brackets in the correct place.

The interviewer talked to Lola (a teenage treasure hunter) about her jungle adventure.

Now try this

1. Rewrite this sentence with the dashes moved to the correct positions.
   The children were scared – and miserable the electricity had gone – off when the storm hit.

2. Insert two commas in the correct places in the sentence below.
   Yasmin Blythe from near Bolton won first prize in the competition.

Had a look ☐   Nearly there ☐   Nailed it! ☐   **Punctuation**

Colons

A **colon** is used to introduce lists and separate independent clauses.

Lists

You can use a colon to introduce a list of items.

> I want to study three subjects: history, maths and science.

← colon

You don't need a capital letter after a colon if the next word wouldn't usually have one.

Example

Insert a colon in the correct place in the sentence below.

I don't like any of Paul's favourite sports: hockey, basketball, karate and swimming.

Independent clauses

After a clause, you can explain what you mean in more detail in another clause. A colon introduces the extra clause.

> My brother was annoyed: we forgot his birthday last week.

first clause — colon — second clause

The second clause **explains** more about the first clause.

Example

Insert a colon in the correct place in the sentence below.

They were late for the match: the bus had broken down.

Now try this

1. Identify the correct colon in the sentence below.
   For his birthday: this is what Dexter wanted: roller skates, a kite, a trampoline: and a cricket bat.
2. How would you rewrite the sentences below to add a colon in the correct place?
   I have lots of hobbies art, netball, reading and dancing.
   After the second heat it was clear Johan was unbeatable.

31

Punctuation — Had a look ☐   Nearly there ☐   Nailed it! ☐

Semi-colons

A **semi-colon** is used to **separate** clauses and items in lists.

Clauses

A semi-colon separates main clauses that are linked in meaning and are equally important.

first main clause   *second main clause*

Shawn loves Italian food   Olivia's favourite dish comes from Thailand
Shawn loves Italian food; Olivia's favourite dish comes from Thailand.

The two clauses can be made into one sentence, separated by the semi-colon.

Both clauses are about the same thing (favourite food) and are equally important.

Items in lists

You should use a semi-colon to separate long **noun phrases** in a list.

See page 2 for more about noun phrases.

colon introduces the list

Use a semi-colon before the final 'and' or 'or'.

Zohar's favourite meals were: spaghetti with cheese sauce; vegetarian sausages with mushrooms and gravy; and spicy chicken noodles.

semi-colons separate the items in the list

Example

Insert a semi-colon in the correct place in the sentence below.

Our team played really badly; we lost the match.

Identify where the first clause ends and the second clause begins. Put the semi-colon between them.

Now try this

1. Identify the correct semi-colon in the sentence below.

   The rain poured down; the rising river; soon burst; its banks

2. Rewrite the sentence below, inserting semi-colons in the correct positions.

   I don't like any of these types of weather: cold, frosty mornings sticky, humid nights never-ending drizzle or baking-hot afternoons in the classroom.

Had a look ☐   Nearly there ☐   Nailed it! ☐   **Punctuation**

Apostrophes: possession

An apostrophe has two important jobs. The first is to show **possession**.

Who does it belong to?

You use an apostrophe to show that something belongs to someone or something. Look at the difference in meaning in this example.

> the lions roar means **the lions are roaring**
> the lion's roar means **the roar of the lion**

Never use an apostrophe to make a noun plural.

Singular or plural?

For singular nouns, including people's names, you add **'s**.
For plural nouns that already end in 's', you only add an apostrophe. You don't need to add another 's'.

singular noun

Giles's grandma didn't want to go to her neighbours' house because of their cat's fleas.

singular noun   *plural noun*

All of these apostrophes show possession.

The words 'children', 'women' and 'men' sound plural but work as singular nouns. So, it is 'the children's toys'.

Example

Insert an apostrophe in the correct place in the sentence below.

The lost keys were in the ladies' suitcase all the time!

The suitcase belongs to the ladies (plural noun ending in s).

Now try this

1. Which of these phrases use the apostrophe correctly?
   - Agnes' mobile
   - the men's changing room
   - Harrys' duck
   - the wolves' territory
   - the women's successes
   - the foxe's den

33

Punctuation   Had a look ☐   Nearly there ☐   Nailed it! ☐

Apostrophes: contraction

The second important job of apostrophes is to show where letters are missing, usually where two words have been made into one.

Missing letters

It is natural to shorten or join words together when we speak or write informally. These are called **contractions**. You use an apostrophe to show exactly where the letters have been omitted (left out). Here are some examples.

I am	we will	it is	you are	do not	should have
I'm	we'll	it's	you're	don't	should've

> You can use contractions in Standard English, but not in formal writing.

Look at the contractions in these sentences.

will not ⟶   ⟵ until

That TV programme <u>won't</u> be on <u>'til</u> nine tonight.
<u>It'd</u> better be worth the wait or I <u>shan't</u> be happy.

It had ⟶   ⟵ shall not

> There are two lots of letters omitted in **shan't** but we don't use two apostrophes (sha'n't).

> Sometimes a single word can be contracted (until → 'til)

> The apostrophes must show exactly where the letters are missing.

Example

Rewrite the sentence below, using the contracted forms of the underlined words.
Fran <u>does not</u> like chips and <u>I would</u> rather not eat broccoli.

Fran <u>doesn't</u> like chips and <u>I'd</u> rather not eat broccoli.

Now try this

1. Correct the contractions in the phrases below.
   - theyl'l be home soon
   - whos' going shopping?
   - its' time for tea
   - wer'e hungry
2. Rewrite the sentence below, using the uncontracted forms of the underlined words.
   <u>I'd</u> like to go swimming, but <u>it'll</u> be too cold and I <u>won't</u> enjoy it.

| Had a look ☐ | Nearly there ☐ | Nailed it! ☐ |

Punctuation

Punctuating speech

When punctuating **direct speech**, it is important you learn exactly where to put the speech marks (inverted commas) and other punctuation marks.

Direct speech

You only ever put the exact words someone says inside a pair of speech marks. Always use a capital letter for the first word spoken. Look carefully at where the speech marks, commas and full stops go.

"My rabbit really likes carrots," said Kirsten.

Anil shouted, "Your parrot is really noisy!"

Don't use two full stops: I said, "Hello." **not** I said, "Hello.".

Reported speech

You may need to change some reported speech into direct speech by adding speech marks, or the other way around.

Reported speech doesn't need speech marks.

Kit said that he would like to visit the steam museum next week.
Kit said, "I would like to visit the steam museum next week."

Direct speech needs speech marks.

Example

Punctuate this sentence to show direct speech.

"What's the problem, Isabella? Hurry up. We need to leave," said Lucy.

Now try this

1. Rewrite the dialogue below, inserting **speech marks**.

   How old are you tomorrow? asked Perry.
   Chris replied, eleven. When's your birthday?
   Not until July! groaned Perry. I can't wait.

Notice that a new line starts when a new person speaks.

35

Punctuation

Had a look ☐   Nearly there ☐   Nailed it! ☐

Hyphens and single dashes

These two punctuation marks look similar but have different jobs.

Hyphens

Hyphens are shorter than dashes and are found **inside** words.

hyphen's job	examples
make meaning clearer	**a little worn dress** (a small dress that is damaged)
	a little-worn dress (a dress that hasn't been worn much)
make compound words	**funny-looking, day-to-day, action-packed**
add the prefixes 're' and 'co' to words starting with a vowel	**re-educate, re-enter, re-energise, co-author, co-ordinate, co-operate**
show word breaks	During the day, the tree frog sleeps on the **under-side** of a leaf in the Amazon.

Single dashes

Sometimes you can use a dash on its own (a pair of dashes is used for a **parenthesis**). A single dash is used in a sentence to show an interruption in speech or thought or a shift of direction.

marks point of interruption

"My homework?" said Jamie. "Sorry, Mrs Harris, I left it on the –"
"Enough! Not that old excuse again!" interrupted his teacher.

The creepy house had been abandoned years ago – at least, that's what they thought.

marks shift in direction to add suspense

Now try this

1. Explain why this newspaper headline is not very clear. Punctuate the sentence to make the meaning clearer.

   Man eating lion spotted lurking in woodland.

2. Rewrite the sentence below to include a single dash.

   You should send a present to your Granny make sure you post it before Tuesday.

Had a look ☐   Nearly there ☐   Nailed it! ☐   **Spelling**

Word families

A **word family** is a group of words that are related to each other in spelling and meaning.

Same root

Words in word families look similar because they share the same **root**.

> act
>
> <u>act</u>ion   re<u>act</u>ive   <u>act</u>or   overre<u>act</u>   inter<u>act</u>   <u>act</u>ivate   in<u>act</u>ive

The root can be found anywhere in the word.

Similar meanings

Words in word families also mean similar things because of their roots.

<u>fact</u>ory	manu<u>fact</u>ure	arte<u>fact</u>	root means **make** or **do**
<u>urb</u>an	con<u>urb</u>ation	sub<u>urb</u>	root means **city**
<u>mar</u>ina	aqua<u>mar</u>ine	<u>mar</u>itime	root means **sea**

Example

*The root is not always spelled the same. Here it's **vinc** and **vic**, which mean conquer.*

Circle the three words from the same word family in the sentence below.

"I am (convinced) that (victory) will be mine for I am (invincible)!"

Now try this

1. Look at the word family below. Does the root <u>view</u> mean **together**, **below**, **see** or **slow**?

    inter<u>view</u>   pre<u>view</u>   re<u>view</u>   <u>view</u>er

2. Find the root that means **build** in the word family below.

    construction   destruct   infrastructure

3. Think of three words that fit in a word family with **miss** as the root.

Spelling   Had a look ☐   Nearly there ☐   Nailed it! ☐

Prefixes

A **prefix** is a group of letters 'fixed' (added) to the beginning of a word.

Prefixes change meaning

When you add a prefix, you change the meaning of the word you are attaching it to (the **root word**). The new word is often opposite or negative in meaning to the root word.

If you don't know what a word in this table means, look it up in a dictionary.

root word	prefix	new word (opposite/negative meaning)
friendly (adverb)	un-	**un**friendly
mortal (adjective)	im-	**im**mortal
fortune (noun)	mis-	**mis**fortune
obey (verb)	dis-	**dis**obey
regular (adjective)	ir-	**ir**regular
logical (adjective)	il-	**il**logical

Never change the spelling of the root word when you add a prefix.

Other prefixes change the meaning but not in an opposite or negative way.

root word	prefix	new word (different meaning)
power (noun)	super-	**super**power
heading (noun)	sub-	**sub**heading
national (adjective)	inter-	**inter**national
angular (adjective)	tri-	**tri**angular
biography (noun)	auto-	**auto**biography
turn (verb)	re-	**re**turn

Learning the meaning of prefixes will help you understand the meaning and spelling of words you don't know.

Example

Attach suitable prefixes to the underlined words in the sentence below to change them to the opposite meaning.

My teacher said that my behaviour was <u>unkind</u>, <u>imperfect</u> and <u>irresponsible</u>.

Now try this

See page 37 for more about root words.

1. Match each prefix to the correct word below to make a new word.

   anti-   im-   bi-   pre-
   cycle   historic   social   perfect

2. Add a prefix to each word below to create a negative or opposite meaning.
   legal   activate   helpful   honest

38

Had a look ☐ Nearly there ☐ Nailed it! ☐   Spelling

Suffixes

A **suffix** is 'fixed' (added) to the end of a word to make a new word.

Making new word classes

Like a prefix, you add a suffix to a root word. You can make nouns, plurals, adjectives, verbs and adverbs as well as change tenses! Here are some examples.

root word	+ suffix	new word
plumb (verb)	+ er	plumb**er** (singular noun)
beauty (noun)	+ ful	beauti**ful** (adjective)
pure (adjective)	+ ify	pur**ify** (verb)
walk (verb)	+ ed	walk**ed** (past tense)
friend (noun)	+ ly	friend**ly** (adverb)

Can you spot the ones where the spelling has changed when the suffix is added?

Recent words

In Years 5 and 6, you will have come across trickier suffixes.

root word	+ suffix	new word
suspicion, ambition	+ cious, + tious	suspi**cious**, ambi**tious**
office, confidence	+ cial, + tial	offi**cial**, confiden**tial**
tolerant, innocent	+ ance, + ence	toler**ance**, inno**cence**
adore	+ able, + ably	ador**able**, ador**ably**
terror	+ ible, + ibly	terr**ible**, terr**ibly**
refer	+ al, + ed, + ing	re<u>ferr</u>**al**, re<u>ferr</u>**ed**, re<u>ferr</u>**ing**
refer	+ ee, + ence	re<u>fer</u>**ee**, re<u>fer</u>**ence**

Example

Don't forget that some suffixes can be just one letter long (y).

Circle the suffixes in the underlined words in the sentence.

It is important that we <u>ident(ify)</u> the <u>guilt(y)</u> person <u>quick(ly)</u>.

Now try this

1. Add an appropriate suffix to each of the nouns below to make adjectives.

   colour   awe   magic   fool   poison   day

| Spelling | Had a look ☐ | Nearly there ☐ | Nailed it! ☐ |

Synonyms and antonyms

Some words have the same meaning and others are opposite in meaning.

Synonyms

You may need to find or use words that have the same or a very similar meaning. These are called **synonyms**.

synonyms: engaging, appealing, striking

Using synonyms can make your own writing more <u>interesting</u> and <u>exciting</u>.

synonyms: lively, dramatic, thrilling

Antonyms

Antonyms are words that have **opposite** meanings.

antonyms: beautiful, attractive

"This place is <u>ugly</u>," <u>whispered</u> Daisy <u>unhappily</u>.

antonyms: shouted, cried

antonyms: cheerfully, joyfully

> Try to use words other than 'said' when you write direct speech. It will make your writing more interesting.

> **Curious** and **odd** are the two adjectives closest in meaning.

Example

Circle two words in the sentence below that are synonyms of each other.

The scientists' latest results were (curious). Something astonishing and very (odd) had happened.

Now try this

1. Identify the pairs of synonyms in the list below.
   free/confined   dismal/bleak   mocking/sarcastic   animated/inactive
2. Replace the underlined adjectives in the sentence below with antonyms.
   The <u>serious</u> play was full of <u>boring</u> characters and <u>ugly</u> scenes.

Had a look ☐   Nearly there ☐   Nailed it! ☐   **Spelling**

Plurals

Plural nouns describe **more than one** of the same thing. They usually end in **-s**, although there are many exceptions.

Making singular nouns plural

The letters at the end of a singular noun often give you a clue about how to write the plural form.

Never use an apostrophe to make a plural noun.

type of word	singular	rule	plural	exceptions!
most nouns	mountain	add s	mountains	
noun ending in s, x, z, ch, sh	glass, box, buzz, inch, dish	add es	glasses, boxes, buzzes, inches, dishes	
noun ending in a **vowel** and y	boy, alley, birthday	add s	boys, alleys, birthdays	
noun ending in a **consonant** and y	party, army, baby	drop the y and add ies	parties, armies, babies	surnames such as 'the Kellys'
noun ending in **f** or **fe**	leaf, knife, half	drop the f or fe and add ves	leaves, knives, halves	roofs, chefs, handcuffs
nouns from other languages ending in **o**	piano, video, kangaroo	add s	pianos, videos, kangaroos	tomatoes, potatoes, heroes

Irregular plurals

Some nouns don't follow any of the rules above. Here are some examples.

man → men   person → people   mouse → mice
child → children   deer → deer   foot → feet

Now try this

See page 1 for more about nouns.

1. Correct the underlined plural nouns in the sentences below.
   We bought two <u>avocado</u>, some <u>strawberrys</u> and three <u>loafs</u> of bread.
   <u>Puppys</u>, <u>kangarooes</u> and <u>fishs</u> are my favourite <u>animales</u>.

41

Spelling Had a look ☐ Nearly there ☐ Nailed it! ☐

Tricky spellings

Some spellings are hard to remember because the same letters make different sounds, or sometimes the letters are even silent!

Silent letters

Some letters in really old words are **no longer sounded out** when we say them today. You must remember to write them though.

All the underlined letters are silent.

> The knight took a solemn vow to return to his island.
>
> I doubt gnomes enjoy eating thistles.

Unstressed vowels

Sometimes you don't fully sound out at the vowels in a word. It sounds like they are not there because they are **unstressed**. Again, you must remember to write them.

All the underlined letters are unstressed.

> In general, I like to try different types of vegetable.
>
> Her business was running frightening tours of the cemetery.

Example

Circle the silent letters or unstressed vowels in the sentence below.

On Wednesday, I saw an interesting show on TV about how to tie knots.

Wednesday has two silent letters: Wednesday.

Now try this

1. Correct the spellings of each of the words below.

   libary   ryme   avrage   hankerchief
   enviroment   musle   defnitely

Had a look ☐   Nearly there ☐   Nailed it! ☐   **Spelling**

More tricky spellings

Some spellings are hard to remember because they are exceptions to the rules, or because the same letters make very different sounds in lots of different words.

'i' before 'e' except after 'c'

In many cases, you spell words putting 'i' before the 'e'.

> field   piece   cashier   diesel   belief   fierce   achieve

This changes when the two letters come directly after a soft 'c' and when the sound they makes is 'ee'.

> ceiling   receipt   deceive   conceit   perceive

There are some exceptions to this rule you should learn.

> seize   weird   protein   either   neither   caffeine

The letter-string 'ough'

The letter-string 'ough' can be used to spell all these different sounds.

'awt'	'uff'	'oh'	'uh'	'ow'	'off'	'oo'
bought	rough	though	thorough	plough	cough	through
thought	tough	dough	borough	bough	trough	

Example

> Weight has an 'ay' sound not an 'ee' sound, so it is not **ie**.

Circle the correct spelling of each underlined word.

Alice's dad put too much wieght / **weight** on the **ceiling** / cieling and came to greif / **grief**.

Now try this

1. Identify the words that rhyme with **tough** in the list below.
   cough   bough   rough   ought   enough   plough

2. Choose the correct spelling of the words in the passage below.
   She seized/siezed her chance to acheive/achieve her dream. Neither/Niether her mother or father could beleive/believe that she would do it.

43

Spelling Had a look ☐ Nearly there ☐ Nailed it! ☐

Homophones

Homophones are words that **sound the same** but are spelled differently and mean different things.

> Leo <u>heard</u> the <u>herd</u> of cattle mooing outside in the lane.
> He <u>guessed</u> that his <u>guest</u> had left the gate open.

Try saying these words. They sound exactly the same.

There are many homophones in English, but here are some you should revise.

there	two	break	peace	whether	allowed
there	to	brake	piece	weather	aloud
they're	too				
past	here	plain	practice (noun)	licence (noun)
passed	hear	plane	practise (verb)	license (verb)

Near homophones

Some words sound <u>almost</u> the same. Again, they have different spellings and meanings.

| quite | effect (noun) | device (noun) | advice (noun) | precede | accept |
| quiet | affect (verb) | devise (verb) | advise (verb) | proceed | except |

Example

Circle the correct near homophone or near homophone to complete the sentence below.

Think carefully about the meaning of the sentence before you choose each word.

Everything was quite / (quiet), (except) / accept for the squeal of the car's breaks / (brakes).

Now try this

1. Choose the correct homophone to complete each sentence below.
   The widow was in *morning / mourning*.
   She walked *past / passed* the bus stop on her way to school.
   The teacher *led / lead* her class out of the school.

44

Had a look ☐   Nearly there ☐   Nailed it! ☐   Writing

Audience and purpose

Before you start writing, you must think about **who** you are writing for (the **audience**) and **what** you are trying to say (the **purpose**).

> You won't have to do a writing test as part of your Year 6 SATs. Your teacher will look at some of your pieces of writing instead. Use the skills in this section to improve your writing.

Audience

Your audience affects the vocabulary and sentence constructions you use.

> The hippo is in the mud. "Mmm, that's cooler," he says. He is a happy hippo.

This is from a picture book for young children. It uses the present tense and short sentences.

> When a hippopotamus is disturbed by an unwary, careless tourist, it may adopt an aggressive, open-mouthed 'yawning' posture, displaying its razor-sharp incisors and tusk-like canines.

This is from a non-fiction text for adults. It uses modal verbs, expanded noun phrases and technical vocabulary.

Purpose

Your purpose will affect the **genre** you choose. For example, are you trying to entertain with a story or are you trying to inform?

> **Tiger behaviour report**
> Tigers drink from crocodile-infested watering holes during the dry season. They are aware of the dangers of crocodiles beneath the water. As they drink, they watch the water surface warily. If attacked, tigers are known to fight back. A tiger will deliberately attack a crocodile's eyes with its claws to disable the crocodile while it escapes.

The purpose of this non-fiction report is to inform. The author has written facts in a neutral way.

Now try this

1. List all of the genres of writing that you know. For each one, write down a description of its audience and its purpose.

45

Writing

Had a look ☐   Nearly there ☐   Nailed it! ☐

Planning and organising

Once you know your audience and the purpose of your writing, you should plan what to write and how to organise it.

Write down your ideas quickly

First remind yourself what you are trying to say. Then think of as many ideas as you can. Single words, spider diagrams, bullet points, quick sketches – anything short and quick will do.

Here is a plan for a review of a film for a school newsletter.

Characters: Jake, Jessie, Captain Bones, Plank
- Great stunts
- Fake effects
- Romance bits disgusting
- Plank very funny
- Bones over the top
- Pirates not scary

Plot – two children race to find treasure on Mars. Defeat gang of space pirates.

Favourite bits
1. Sword fight
2. Cliff chase
3. Jokes

Too long (2.5 hours!)   12A   2/5 stars   Don't bother!   Music dramatic   Sound effects too loud

Don't write in detail. Just write enough to remind you of your ideas.

Organise your plan into a logical sequence

Organise your work so that it is logical and easy to follow. Use **paragraphs** to structure your work. Each paragraph should have a **central idea** or **theme**.

Paragraph theme	Should contain	Notes from plan
Basic information	Name, genre, length, age rating	Pirates on Mars, sci-fi comedy, 2.5 hours, 12A
Plot	Brief outline of the story	Two children race to find treasure on Mars. Defeat gang of space pirates.
Characters	Brief details of main characters	Jake, Jessie, Captain Bones (over the top), Plank (very funny)
Sound	My opinion of the music and sound	Music dramatic, sound effects too loud
Likes	What I particularly liked	Great stunts, sword fight, cliff chase, jokes
Dislikes	Anything I didn't like	Fake effects, romance bits disgusting, pirates not scary
Conclusion	My overall opinion	2/5 stars, don't bother

Now try this

1. Write a review of a book you have recently read, using appropriate paragraph themes.

Had a look ☐   Nearly there ☐   Nailed it! ☐   Writing

Writing and editing

In an assessment, you should stick to your plan. Edit and improve your writing as you go.

Top writing tips

Here's how to stay on course as you write.

Do ✓	Don't ✗
Keep your audience in mind at all times.	
Follow an organised plan.	Don't make it all up as you go along.
Keep to the subject.	Don't repeat the same points.
Include the features and style of your genre.	Don't change genre halfway through.
Expand the ideas on your plan as you go if you have time.	Don't run out of ideas and stop writing. Look at your plan again and think of more.
Capture the reader's interest with your sentence starters.	
Use a wide range of vocabulary, sentence constructions and punctuation.	Don't write one long paragraph.
Use paragraphs in a logical order.	Don't muddle up your points.
Link ideas within paragraphs, using connectives and adverbials.	
Link paragraphs using appropriate words and phrases.	
Give examples to support your points.	

Edit as you go

You will not have time to write rough work and then write a clean version. You should add, delete or change what you have written as you work.

At this stage, you are not checking your work; you are improving it.

original sentences

~~Jasmina woke up early. She would never have survived otherwise.~~
Luckily, Jasmina woke up early. *She would never have survived ~~otherwise~~.
*Three more minutes in bed and she

Try to keep your changes as neat as possible.

added adverb and punctuation   added phrase for emphasis   neat deletion

Now try this

1. Copy and edit the sentence below to improve it.

   The bull ran towards the walkers.

47

Writing   Had a look ☐   Nearly there ☐   Nailed it! ☐

Checking

When you finish writing, check your work and correct any mistakes.

The big picture

> Have you written in a style and genre suitable for your audience and purpose?
> If not, edit your word choice and features.

> Have you followed your plan?
> If not, add more to a paragraph or write a new one.

> Have you repeated points or added detail you don't need?
> If you have, remove repetition.

> Are your ideas organised into paragraphs in a logical order?
> If not, circle text you want to move and use an arrow to show where it should go.

Proofreading

Check your spelling, grammar and punctuation thoroughly. Use the questions below to check each sentence.

- Have I used a capital letter at the beginning and for proper nouns?
- Have I used a full stop, question mark or exclamation mark at the end?
- Have I placed speech marks around direct speech?
- Have I placed commas correctly in lists and around clauses?
- Have I placed apostrophes correctly to show possession or contraction?

Now try this

1. Proofread the passage below. Copy it out, correcting the mistakes.

   during queen victorias reign young lads called mudlarks waded at low tide in the filthy mud of the river thames wear they searched for scraps of led iron and other waist to cell

Had a look ☐   Nearly there ☐   Nailed it! ☐   Writing

Writing articles

Articles are written for newspapers, magazines, websites and blogs.

Look!

Articles need to grab the reader's attention and keep them reading.

The **opening paragraph** summarises the story.

Paragraphs are short and stick to the point.

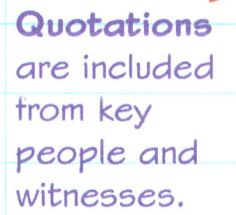

Quotations are included from key people and witnesses.

The News

Monday, 8th August

The News

HOME   LOCAL   WORLD   SPORT   SCIENCE   GALLERY

Music misery for moles

Reporter: Meggie Long

Music from a drum and bass festival in Surrey is distressing moles and driving them from their natural habitat, according to scientists. The organisers of D&B Fest deny the claim.

The popular festival takes place over four days every July. Dr Saffron Baffin claims that the bass notes cause vibrations that travel far underground. These vibrations confuse and distress the moles in their burrows.

"Using underground cameras and GPS tracking, I've observed the moles becoming lost and even fighting each other in their confusion. Many become exhausted as they dig frantically away from the music," said the ecologist from the University of Southern England.

Other scientists confirm that the local mole population has declined.

D&B Fest says that the noise is not the problem. Instead, organisers claim, the large local population of buzzards is to blame.

The festival promoter explained, "Our scientists tell us the moles are being eaten by birds of prey when they come to the surface. We're not responsible for that."

It seems that local residents have mixed feelings. Keen gardener Leon Tanner, 73, noted, "I don't like that so-called music, but now the moles have gone, my lawn has never looked so good."

The **headline** is eye-catching and alliterative.

The **byline** explains who wrote the article.

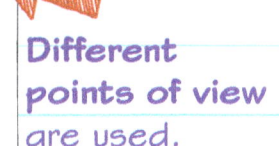

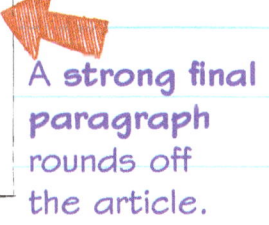

Different points of view are used.

A **strong final paragraph** rounds off the article.

See page 35 for more about punctuating speech.

Now try this

1. Imagine you are a journalist. You have been asked to write a newspaper article on the development of a new skate park. The new skate park will replace a small, quiet, green area mainly used by families, dog walkers and elderly people. Plan and write your article. Use the layout above, the features listed and your imagination!

49

Writing | Had a look ☐ | Nearly there ☐ | Nailed it! ☐

Writing explanations

This type of text is used to explain **how** something works or **why** something happens.

Step-by-step process

The purpose of an explanation is to describe a process clearly. The order of your pieces of information and how they are linked are very important.

Title uses **how** to state what is being explained.

Conjunctions such as **first** help explain in which order things happen.

Present tense verbs explain the process as if it is happening now.

Important technical vocabulary is explained.

Conjunctions such as **then** link the steps in the process.

An interesting fact holds the reader's attention.

HOW A DIGITAL CAMERA WORKS

First, light travels from the scene in front of the camera to the lens. The lens focuses the light onto a small sensor. The light hits the whole surface area of the sensor.

The sensor is divided into millions of tiny squares called pixels. Each pixel produces a particular electric charge, depending on the colour and brightness of the light that hits it. The microchip in the camera then converts the grid of millions of different charges into an image file. This file is then stored on a memory card and can be displayed on the camera screen. Later, it can be uploaded to a computer. Because the picture consists of digital information (pixels), it can also be edited and shared electronically.

The most powerful digital camera in the world is being built in Chile. It will be used to photograph the night sky. The sensor will take 3,200-megapixel images.

33

See page 14 for more about conjunctions.

Now try this

1. Write an explanation of how a toaster works. Use the features shown in the example.

50

Had a look ☐   Nearly there ☐   Nailed it! ☐

Writing

Writing persuasive letters

A letter can be **formal** or **informal**, depending on your audience. You write a persuasive letter to someone to **convince** them about something.

A formal letter

Look carefully at the language and layout of this letter. Sanjay has written it to persuade his head teacher to let him and a friend camp on the school field.

Write the name, title and address of the person to whom you are writing.

25 London Lane
Lower Brooktown
LB7 4YA
20th June

Your address

Ms Mellor
Head teacher
Grantbury Primary School
Grantbury
GR4 9GC

Use their title and name if you know it. Otherwise, use 'Sir or Madam'.

Dear Ms Mellor,

Re: Camping on the school field

This is what the letter is about.

I am writing to request that you allow my friend Will and me to camp on the school field for one night next week.

We are both keen astronomers and we are very excited about the meteor shower that should take place in the middle of the night next Wednesday.

Neither Will nor I live somewhere suitable to watch the display: we both live in streets where there is too much light. The school field is not polluted by light in the same way and it would be the perfect place to set up our telescopes. The fence would also make us feel much more secure.

We will be taking HD photos of the sky and I would like to offer you a framed print as a thank you. We will also be live-blogging our experience and we will, of course, mention what a wonderful school we go to. Finally, we are hoping to find a new planet, which we will name Melloria in your honour.

I would be grateful if you would grant my request and I look forward to your reply.

Yours sincerely,

Sanjay Desai

Mr Sanjay Desai

Use a logical sequence of paragraphs.

Give persuasive reasons.

Say what you hope will happen next.

Write **Yours sincerely** when you know the person to whom you are writing. Otherwise, write **Yours faithfully**.

Write your signature.

Clearly write your title and full name.

Now try this

See page 25 for more about Standard English.

1. List the arguments Sanjay makes to persuade his head teacher. Can you think of any more arguments he could have included?

51

Writing | Had a look ☐ Nearly there ☐ Nailed it! ☐

Writing balanced arguments

In a balanced argument, you must give **both points of view**.

For and against

Should children be allowed to use screens for only one hour per day? ← question as title

Many children argue with their parents about how much time they spend on their mobile phones. The Prime Minister has suggested that there should be a law to restrict 'screen time' to one hour a day for every child in the country. ← short introduction that explains the issue

<u>Firstly</u>, many parents will agree with this idea as they think their children should be reading or playing with their friends instead. ← first point for, introduced by a conjunction

<u>Secondly</u>, parents also complain that their children become antisocial and cannot control their screen time. <u>Consequently</u>, they believe it damages family life and support the Prime Minister's plan. ← further points for, introduced or linked by conjunctions

<u>On the other hand</u>, children argue that they may be reading an eBook or playing a game with friends. ← first point against

<u>Furthermore</u>, they claim they are not being antisocial because they are communicating with their friends electronically. <u>In addition</u>, many children say that they regulate their 'screen time' themselves. They claim a one-hour restriction would punish those who do not overuse their devices. ← further points against

<u>In conclusion</u>, there are good arguments for restricting 'screen time', especially for those children who can't restrict themselves. However, <u>on balance</u>, I believe a one-hour time limit is too restrictive and unfair. ← The conclusion sums up the argument. You can include your own views.

Now try this

1. Write down one more point for and one more point against the argument in the text above.

52

Had a look ☐   Nearly there ☐   Nailed it! ☐   Writing

Writing stories

You can use a short piece of text or a picture as inspiration for writing your own story. For example, you could write a **short story**, using this as the beginning.

← first person   past tense →

> I put the key in the lock and twisted it anticlockwise. The rusty mechanism squealed in protest. I turned the handle, put my shoulder to the wood and pushed, flattening the long grass at the bottom. The strange door opened.

↖ clue about   ↖ clue about the mood
the setting   of the writing

Freedom and focus

A story can be fun to write as you are free to use your imagination. It can also be difficult because you might lose focus. Make decisions before you start. Look for clues in the question.

Before you start writing

- Decide **where** the action will take place (the **setting**).
- Decide **when** the action will take place. Does it happen in modern times, the future or a time in history?
- Decide **what** is going to happen (the **plot**). Decide how the story will end.
- Decide **who** is going to be in your story (the **characters**). Don't use more than three characters.

When you are writing

- Do not change the **tense**.
- Use **paragraphs** to separate the main events.
- Use words and phrases to link your paragraphs and make the story flow.
- Use a mixture of action, description and direct speech. Do not just list the things that happen.

> See page 8 for more about the past tense.

Now try this

1. Continue the story at the top of this page.

Reading — Had a look ☐   Nearly there ☐   Nailed it! ☐

Reading skills: close meaning

Sometimes you need to look in detail at certain words or phrases and their meaning. You will need to **scan** the text to find certain things.

Skill 1: find information

You will need to find key details in fiction and non-fiction texts. This may mean finding a single word or a phrase.

> See page 61 for more about finding information.

Skill 2: explain the meaning

Some questions ask you to explain what a word means or choose words or phrases with a similar meaning. Think about the **context** (what comes before and after the word) to help you work out what the word means.

> The judge threw the <u>case</u> out of court.

Here **case** means a legal investigation, not the judge's suitcase!

Skill 3: explain word choice

> See page 72 for more about author's language.

You will be asked to explain how the words used add to the meaning of the writing. You might need to find words the author uses to create a certain effect.

Skill 4: make inferences

You make inferences when you use clues in the text to figure out things the author hasn't told you directly. You need to provide evidence from the text to support your inferences.

> See page 69 for more about inferences.

Example

What inference could you make from this sentence?
John studied his daughter's guilty face angrily: there were crumbs on her lips and dark brown smears around her mouth.

The words **crumbs**, **dark brown smears** and **guilty** are strong clues.

You could infer that John's daughter has eaten chocolate biscuits or cake when she wasn't supposed to.

Had a look ☐   Nearly there ☐   Nailed it! ☐   Reading

Reading skills: the whole text

Some questions focus on 'the big picture'. You will have to think about the whole text. It is a good idea to **skim read** the text first before you read it through carefully.

Skill 5: summarise

> See page 63 for more about summarising.

A summary states the main points in a text. You may need to identify the main message in more than one paragraph or put some events in the right order.

Skill 6: make predictions

> See page 70 for more about predicting.

Some questions will ask you to make a prediction about what happens next. Think about what has already happened and how the characters might behave.

Example

Use clues from this sentence to continue the story.
John angrily studied his daughter's guilty face: there were crumbs on her lips and dark brown smears around her mouth.

> We know John is reacting angrily and his daughter feels guilty. This means she probably feels upset.

John lost his temper and told his daughter off for eating the biscuits. Her bottom lip started to quiver.

Skill 7: explain how things are related

You may need to explain the theme of a story or explain how different pieces of information in a non-fiction text create the overall meaning of the whole text.

Skill 8: make comparisons

> See page 67 for more about themes.

Some questions will ask you to compare information, characters or events from different parts of the text. For example, you may be asked to explain how a character's mood changes.

> See page 66 for more about character.

Now try this

1. Create a poster explaining these skills in your own words.

Question types: selected answers

Follow the instructions carefully

*Pay extra attention to words in **bold**.*

For some questions, you will not need to write anything. You will have to tick or circle your answer or draw lines.

For these questions, you need to **select** answers from a number of choices. Here are two examples.

Match the events below to the year in which they happened.

Draw neat lines and match up your answers clearly.

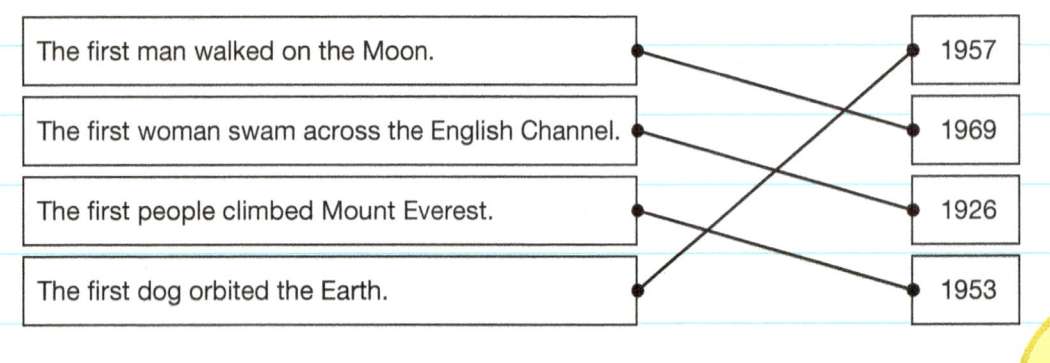

The first man walked on the Moon.	—	1957
The first woman swam across the English Channel.	—	1969
The first people climbed Mount Everest.	—	1926
The first dog orbited the Earth.	—	1953

(The first man walked on the Moon → 1969; The first woman swam across the English Channel → 1926; The first people climbed Mount Everest → 1953; The first dog orbited the Earth → 1957)

Tick one box in each row to show whether each statement is a **fact** or an **opinion**.

Look at the instructions. Make sure you tick one box in each row.

	Fact	Opinion
Alice in Wonderland is a fiction book.	✓	
Dr Seuss is a better writer than Roald Dahl.		✓
The Three Little Pigs are annoying and deserve to be eaten.		✓
Winnie-the-Pooh is a bear.	✓	

Now try this

1. Tick one box in each row to show whether each statement is **fact** or **opinion**.

	Fact	Opinion
Video games are available for a range of consoles.		
Children play too many video games now.		
People can win awards for video games, just like for films.		

Had a look ☐   Nearly there ☐   Nailed it! ☐   **Reading**

Question types: free answers

Some questions are followed by a box or some lines. This shows what type of answer is needed. You will need to use **evidence** from the text to support your answer.

Short answers

Some questions are followed by a short line or a few lines.

> Who visits Narnia first?

__Lucy__   ← The short line shows that you only need to write a word or a few words.

> How and when did Ray Tomlinson make history?

__He was the first person to send an email.__
__He sent it in 1971.__

← These two lines show that you should write a few words or a sentence or two.

Longer answers

Some questions are followed by a large box.

> Describe the character of Snow White's stepmother, the Queen.

__She is vain as she is always asking the mirror how__
__beautiful she is. She is also jealous of Snow White's__
__beauty. Finally, she is untrustworthy and cruel as she__
__disguises herself and poisons Snow White with an apple.__

← Support your answer with evidence from the text. You need to show how you know she is vain or cruel, using examples of her behaviour.

Now try this

1. How would you describe a car to someone who had never seen one? Write a four-line description.

57

Reading

Non-fiction text

Read this non-fiction text about 'alien invaders'.

Alien Invaders!

Believe it or not, there are tens of thousands of aliens invading all parts of planet Earth and doing billions of pounds' worth of damage. Now, these organisms may not technically be from outer space, but they're definitely in the wrong place.

When an animal or plant moves from its natural habitat to a new area, scientists class the organism as an 'alien invasive species'. Such species can have devastating effects on the native plants and animals in their new homes.

How do the invasive species spread?

Human behaviour is often to blame. Some invaders are spread from one continent to another by the global food and pet trade. Some species 'hitchhike' on the hulls of ships or in their ballast water. Sometimes people introduce a new animal into a habitat to try to solve a problem caused by an existing species. This often makes things worse!

Did you know?
The golden apple snail was brought from Latin America to Asia in the 1980s as a gourmet food. However, the snails weren't popular with diners, so the snails and their eggs were released into lakes and rivers. The species then spread to a dozen countries, causing huge damage to rice crops in the paddy fields.

The snail lays its eggs above the waterline to protect them from fish.

Australia's deadly cane toads

One of the most notorious invasive species is the cane toad. Cane toads were introduced from South and Central America in the 1930s to control the pest beetles that were damaging the sugar cane crops in Queensland, Australia.

Because they have no natural predators in Australia, the toads have since spread rapidly into other parts of the country and their numbers have surged. As the toads move into new areas, the native animals that normally eat frogs eat the toads and are poisoned.

Cane toad (Rhinella marina)

Cane toad fact file
Name Cane toad (*Rhinella marina*)
Description Large, tough amphibian; average weight of 1.8 kg; warty skin; webbed back feet
Behaviour Greedy predator of insects and other small prey, but will even eat pet food; night-forager; ground-dwelling; needs constant access to moisture to survive; doesn't drink but absorbs water through the skin on its belly
Impact Produces a milky toxin from the glands on its upper surface for defence; predators die quickly if they eat a toad as the poison causes heart failure
Population About 200 million; females lay between 8,000 and 30,000 eggs at a time in still or slow-moving water; toadlets reach adult size within a year; species is spreading across Australia by 40 to 60 km per year

How can an invasive species be stopped?

People have to work hard to deal with the damage caused by invasive species. Australians have come up with a number of clever and radical solutions to manage the cane toad menace.

Solution	Description
Culling	Because the cane toad is regarded as a major environmental pest, community volunteers often take part in large-scale culls.
	Every March in Queensland, there is a pest control event called Toad Day Out. The cane toads are captured alive and unharmed. There are prizes for the heaviest toads and for the schools that catch the most. The toads are examined by experts and then destroyed. However, there are still arguments about the most humane way to do this.
Fine-mesh fences	According to new research, building special fences around artificial water sources in dry parts of Australia could help deal with the spread of cane toads.
	The toads are attracted to the water but they can't climb over the fences or dig under them. They die in large numbers because the fences hold them back. Livestock farmers discovered that the fences were effective at keeping the toad populations down: about 100 times more toads were found at unfenced pools than at fenced ones. As well as building the fences, farmers are being encouraged to use water tanks instead of dams for their cattle.
Lizard training	Some native animals have been trained not to eat the toads.
	In Australia, wild monitor lizards are called goannas. Researchers discovered that it only takes 30 seconds of chewing a toad to kill a goanna. The researchers trained a population of yellow-spotted monitor lizards by feeding each one a small, young toad from a fishing pole. The lizards were sick, but survived. The scientists then attached radio transmitters to them. Their observations showed that many of the goannas remembered their nasty experience. The team also tracked lots of untrained goannas. These monitors were all dead within a few months of the toads invading.

Yellow-spotted monitor lizard

Reading — Had a look ☐ Nearly there ☐ Nailed it! ☐

Non-fiction features

Non-fiction texts such as **explanations**, **articles** and **reports** have special features you don't usually find in fiction.

Reports

See pages 58–59 for Alien Invaders!

A report is a piece of writing full of facts about a particular topic. A report has a **title** and an **introduction**. The writer uses **sub-headings** to organise the information into sections.

sub-heading to introduce new section →

paragraph about where the toads came from →

paragraph about how the toads have spread →

> **Australia's deadly cane toads**
>
> One of the most notorious invasive species is the cane toad. Cane toads were introduced from South and Central America in the 1930s to control the pest beetles that were damaging the sugar cane crops in Queensland, Australia.
>
> Because they have no natural predators in Australia, the toads have since spread rapidly into other parts of the country and their numbers have surged.

The language in a report is usually formal.

Explanations

Explanations are similar to reports but they also explain how or why something happens. The language is formal and may include **technical vocabulary**.

Paragraph explains **how** the fences work →

> The toads are attracted to the water but they can't climb over the fences or dig under them. They die in large numbers because the fences hold them back. <u>Livestock farmers</u> discovered that the fences were effective at keeping the <u>toad populations</u> down ...

↑ technical vocabulary

Now try this

1. Research an animal from *Alien Invaders!* Write an report on its life cycle.

Had a look ☐   Nearly there ☐   Nailed it! ☐   **Reading**

Retrieving and recording

You need to be able to **retrieve** (find) information from the text and **record** it (write it down).

These questions test your ability to find information.

Scanning the text

The quickest way to find information is to **scan** the text. Remember, you are looking for a specific fact.

See page 54, Skill 1.

Scan the text for specific words relevant to the question.

Question: In which decade were cane toads introduced to Australia?

> One of the most notorious invasive species is the cane toad. They were introduced from South and Central America in the 1930s to control the pest beetles.

Answer: in the 1930s

Finding more than one example

Some questions ask you to find more than one example from the text.

Question: According to the text, how do invasive species spread? Give **two** examples.

> Human behaviour is often to blame. Some invaders are spread from one continent to another by the global food and pet trade. Some species 'hitchhike' on the hulls of ships or in their ballast water.

There are lots of different reasons that you could give.

Answer: 1. in ship's ballast water 2. due to the global food and pet trade

Now try this

Answer these questions about *Alien Invaders!* on pages 58–59.
1. When is the Toad Day Out event held in Queensland?
2. Why was the Golden Apple Snail introduced to Asia?

61

Reading | Had a look ☐ | Nearly there ☐ | Nailed it! ☐

Point, Evidence, Explain (PEE)

How to use PEE

Here is an extract from *Alien Invaders!* on pages 58–59.

See page 54, Skill 4.

> The scientists then attached radio transmitters to them. Their observations showed that many of the goannas had remembered their nasty experience.

Question: Was the lizard training successful?

It was successful in many cases. ← You should start by making your **point** refer back to the question.

The researchers reported that "many of the goannas remembered their nasty experience". ← Then, you need to provide **evidence** from the text to support your point. You should use quotation marks around any words you copy from the text.

This means that many of the monitor lizards now avoided eating cane toads and so were not poisoned. ← Finally, **explain** what your evidence proves.

Final answer:

It was successful in many cases. The researchers reported that "many of the goannas remembered their nasty experience". This means that many of the monitor lizards now avoided eating cane toads and so were not poisoned.

Now try this

1. Read *Alien Invaders!* on pages 58–59. Which solution to the cane toad problem do you think is most cruel to the invaders? Use PEE to support your answer.

Had a look ☐ Nearly there ☐ Nailed it! ☐ **Reading**

Summarising

A summary gathers together the main points in a piece of writing.

What's the message?

See page 55, Skill 5.

You may be asked about the main message or ideas of the text. You will need to **summarise** the text in your head before you select your answer. If you are not sure, skim the text again to get a general feeling.

> What is the main message of the *Alien Invaders!* report?

strong clue that the question is testing your summarising skills

overall point of the report

Tick **one**.

Invasive species cannot be controlled.	☐
People should be more careful about releasing snails.	☐
Native species are to blame. They should fight back.	☐
People must work hard to protect native species.	✓

True or false?

The same question might be asked in a different way, but you will still need to think of the text as a whole.

strong clue that the question is testing your summarising skills

> Thinking about the text as a whole, tick one box in each row to show whether each statement is **true** or **false**?

	True	False
Invasive species cannot be controlled.		✓
People should be more careful about releasing snails.	✓	
Native species are to blame. They should fight back.		✓
People must work hard to protect native species.	✓	

There is evidence across lots of different paragraphs for these answers.

Now try this

1. Find out about another invasive species. Write a short paragraph summarising what you discovered.

Reading

Fiction text

This is an extract from *A Wrinkle in Time* by Madeleine L'Engle, a science-fiction fantasy written in 1963. It tells the story of Meg (Margaret) and her brother Charles who go on a dangerous journey across space and time.

In her attic bedroom Margaret Murry, wrapped in an old patchwork quilt, sat on the foot of her bed and watched the trees tossing in the frenzied lashing of the wind. Behind the trees clouds scudded frantically across the sky. Every few moments the moon ripped through them, creating wraith-like shadows that raced along the ground.

The house shook.

Wrapped in her quilt, Meg shook.

She wasn't usually afraid of the weather.
It's not just the weather, she thought.
– It's the weather on top of everything else.
On top of me. On top of Meg Murry doing everything wrong.

School. School was all wrong. She'd been dropped down to the lowest section in her grade. That morning one of her teacher had said crossly, "Really, Meg, I don't understand how a child with parents as brilliant as yours are supposed to be can be such a poor student. If you don't manage to do a little better you'll have to stay back next year."

During lunch she'd fooled around a little to try to make herself feel better, and one of the girls said scornfully, "After all, Meg, we aren't babies anymore. Why do you always act like one?"

And on the way home from school, walking up the road with her arms full of books, one of the boys had said something about her "dumb baby brother". At this she'd thrown the books on the side of the road and tackled him with every ounce of strength she had, and arrived home with her blouse torn and a big bruise under one eye.

Sandy and Dennys, her ten-year-old twin brothers, who got home from school an hour earlier than she did, were disgusted. "Let us do the fighting when it's necessary," they told her.

– A delinquent, that's what I am, she thought grimly. – That's what they'll be saying next. Not mother. But them. Everybody else. I wish father –

But it was still not possible to think about her father without the danger of tears. Only her mother could talk about him in a natural way, saying, "When your father gets back –"

Gets back from where? And when? Surely her mother must know what people were saying, must be aware of the smugly vicious gossip. Surely it must hurt her as it did Meg. But if it did she gave no outward sign. Nothing ruffled the serenity of her expression.

– Why can't I hide it, too? Meg thought. Why do I always have to *show* everything?

The window rattled madly in the wind, and she pulled the quilt close about her. Curled up on one of her pillows a grey fluff of kitten yawned, showing its pink tongue, tucked its head under again, and went back to sleep.

Everybody was asleep. Everybody except Meg. Even Charles Wallace, the "dumb baby brother", who had an uncanny way of knowing when she was awake and unhappy, and who would come, so many nights, tiptoeing up the attic stairs to her – even Charles Wallace was asleep.

How could they sleep? All day on the radio there had been hurricane warnings. How could they leave her up in the attic in the rickety brass bed, knowing that the roof might be blown off the house, and she tossed out into the wild night sky to land who knows where?

Her shivering grew uncontrollable.

– You asked to have the attic bedroom, she told herself savagely. – Mother let you have it because you're the oldest. It's a privilege, not a punishment.

"Not during a hurricane, it isn't a privilege," she said aloud. She tossed the quilt down on the foot of the bed, and stood up. The kitten stretched luxuriously, and looked at her with huge, innocent eyes.

"Go back to sleep," Meg said. "Just be glad you're a kitten and not a monster like me."

Reading

Had a look ☐   Nearly there ☐   Nailed it! ☐

Character

Characters are people in a story. The word **character** can also mean a person's personality and appearance.

> See pages 54–55, Skill 2, 4 and 6.

Character clues

Writers often describe their characters through their **actions**, **speech** and **thoughts**, not just what they look like. Here are some examples from *A Wrinkle in Time* (pages 64–65).

> Why can't I hide it, too? Meg thought. Why do I always have to show everything?

The author describes Meg's **thoughts**. We understand from this that Meg tends to 'show' her emotions. She wishes she could 'hide' her feelings.

> Sandy and Dennys, her ten-year-old twin brothers, who got home from school an hour earlier than she did, were disgusted. "Let us do the fighting when it's necessary," they told her.

The author uses **speech** to show that Meg's brothers don't like Meg fighting and that they think it's their duty.

> Charles Wallace… who had an uncanny way of knowing when she was awake and unhappy and who would come, so many nights, tiptoeing up the attic stairs to her…

The author describes Charles's **actions**: the mysterious way he senses Meg's mood even when they are not in the same room. You can make the **inference** that Charles might have an unusual ability and that he and Meg have a close relationship.

Example

> The word <u>savagely</u> means angrily.

Underline a word in this sentence that suggests Meg gets cross about things.

You asked to have the attic bedroom, she told herself <u>savagely</u>.

Now try this

> See page 69 for more about inference.

1. Based on the extract, write a brief description of Meg's character.

66

Had a look ☐   Nearly there ☐   Nailed it! ☐   **Reading**

Theme

The **theme** of a story is the **main idea** or **message** that runs through it.

Sequences and patterns

See page 55, Skill 7.

In the reading test, you may be asked to explain how ideas and events are related to create a theme. You will need to look for **sequences of events** or **patterns of ideas**. You might need to make inferences.

One of the themes of the extract from *A Wrinkle in Time* (pages 64–65) is Meg's bad day.

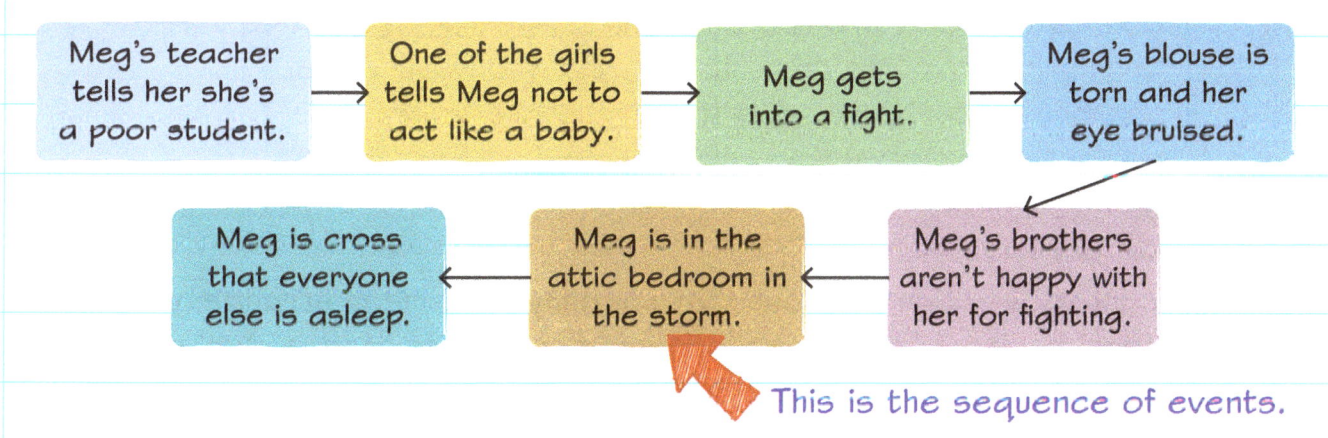

Meg's teacher tells her she's a poor student. → One of the girls tells Meg not to act like a baby. → Meg gets into a fight. → Meg's blouse is torn and her eye bruised.

Meg is cross that everyone else is asleep. ← Meg is in the attic bedroom in the storm. ← Meg's brothers aren't happy with her for fighting.

This is the sequence of events.

Another theme of the extract from *A Wrinkle in Time* is **family relationships**.

This is the pattern of ideas.

Evidence or inference from the text	This helps show...
Meg isn't clever like her parents.	Meg's relationship with her parents.
Meg gets into a fight.	Meg is protective of Charles.
Meg nearly cries.	Meg is missing her father.
Meg thinks about Charles's uncanny ability.	Meg and Charles have a close relationship.
Meg has the attic bedroom.	Meg's mother makes decisions.

See page 69 for more about inference.

Now try this

1. The extract is at the start of the story. Based on what you've read, what other themes will be in the rest of the story?

67

Reading | Had a look ☐ | Nearly there ☐ | Nailed it! ☐

Finding meaning

Some questions ask you to give or explain the meaning of a word or phrase.

Context

> See page 54, Skill 2.

Many words have more than one meaning. The key to understanding the meaning of a word is to look at the **context** (the words surrounding it).

What is the meaning of the word **uncanny**?

← the mystery word

→ This means he can tell when she's awake and unhappy.

> Charles Wallace…who had an uncanny way of knowing when she was awake and unhappy, and who would come, so many nights, tiptoeing up the attic stairs to her…

↑ This means he's coming from a different room.

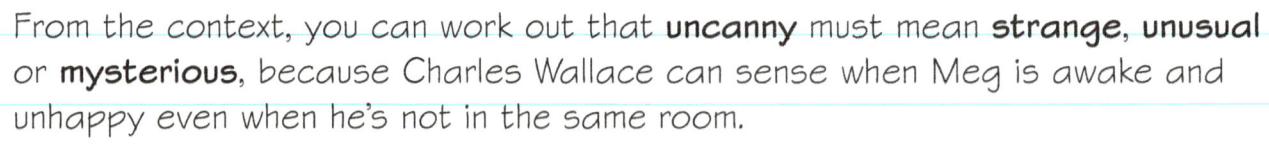

From the context, you can work out that **uncanny** must mean **strange**, **unusual** or **mysterious**, because Charles Wallace can sense when Meg is awake and unhappy even when he's not in the same room.

Synonyms

Sometimes you will need to identify words that are close in meaning.

> The kitten stretched **luxuriously**, and looked at her with huge, innocent eyes.

The word **luxuriously** is closest in meaning to…

- quickly ☐
- expensively ☐
- fully ✓
- nervously ☐

> Luxury can mean expensive, but here *luxuriously* means that kitten has a long, full stretch.

> See page 40 for more about synonyms.

Now try this

> Turn back to A Wrinkle in Time on pages 64–65 to look at the context.

1. Choose the word that is closest in meaning to *delinquent*.

   hero   coward   crook   wrongdoer

Had a look ☐   Nearly there ☐   Nailed it! ☐   **Reading**

Inference

Writers do not always tell you everything in an obvious way. Instead, you have to 'read between the lines'.

> Some questions will ask you to make inferences.

Reading between the lines

When you figure something out from clues in the text, you are making an **inference**.

> See page 54, Skill 4.

> In her attic bedroom Margaret Murry, wrapped in an old patchwork quilt, sat on the foot of her bed and watched the <u>trees tossing</u> in the <u>frenzied lashing</u> of the wind. Behind the trees <u>clouds scudded frantically</u> across the sky.

The author uses some vivid language (such as **trees tossing**) to paint a picture of violent weather. Although the author doesn't say it directly, we can make the inference that there is a powerful storm.

> The window rattled madly in the wind, and she pulled the quilt close about her. <u>Curled up</u> on one of her pillows a grey fluff of kitten <u>yawned</u>, showing its pink tongue, tucked its head under again, and went <u>back to sleep</u>.

The paragraph describes how the kitten wakes up for a moment. The author never says that the kitten isn't scared but we understand that it's not bothered by the storm from its casual behaviour.

Example

How does Meg's kitten react to the storm outside?

The kitten is not worried as it's curled up asleep, yawns and goes back to sleep again.

> We read between the lines that 'curled up', 'yawned' and 'back to sleep' are signs the kitten is not bothered by the storm.

Now try this

> Don't guess. Always look for clues in the text.

Read the extract from *A Wrinkle in Time* on pages 64–65.
1. How does Meg feel on her way back from school?
2. Why does Meg feel upset when she thinks about her father?

69

Reading | Had a look ☐ Nearly there ☐ Nailed it! ☐

Predicting

You make a **prediction** when you explain what you think will happen next.

What's already happened?

See page 55, Skill 6.

You can't just make up the next part of the story. You must think about what's come before, and use reasons from the text to explain your prediction. The extract from *A Wrinkle in Time* (pages 64–65) ends like this.

> You asked to have the attic bedroom, she told herself savagely. – Mother let you have it because you're the oldest. It's a privilege, not a punishment.
>
> "Not during a hurricane, it isn't a privilege," she said aloud. She tossed the quilt down on the foot of the bed, and stood up. The kitten stretched luxuriously, and looked at her with huge, innocent eyes.
>
> "Go back to sleep," Meg said. "Just be glad you're a kitten and not a monster like me."

1. Meg is cross with herself.
2. She doesn't want to be in the attic.
3. She gets up in a temper.
4. She is feeling negative.

Look for clues in the text to help you make your prediction.

Example

Quote words or phrases from the text as evidence for your prediction.

What do these paragraphs suggest might happen next? Use evidence from these paragraphs to support your prediction.

I predict that she will go to her baby brother's room. She is cross and upset, stuck all alone in the attic in the storm. She tells herself off "savagely" for wanting the attic bedroom and calls herself a "monster" so she might want someone to cheer her up.

Now try this

Who might Meg see? How might they react?

1. Based on what you have read, what might happen to Meg next? You can use your imagination but use the clues in the text to help you.

70

Had a look ☐   Nearly there ☐   Nailed it! ☐

Reading

Making comparisons

Some questions will ask you to look for differences or changes in the text.

Differences

See page 55, Skill 8.

You may have to **compare** information, characters or events. This means you need to find differences.

Question: Compare how Meg and her mother feel about the father's disappearance.

*You will need to find **evidence** from different paragraphs to support your answer.*

Evidence:

> **Meg:** …it was still not possible to think about her father without the danger of tears…
>
> **Mother:** …she gave no outward sign. Nothing ruffled the serenity of her expression…

Quote words or phrases directly from the text.

Answer: Meg is upset when she thinks of her father. She is in "danger of tears". Her mother does not seem affected. She has a "serene" expression and shows no "outward sign" of being upset.

Changes

You may also have to explain **changes** within the text.

Example

You need to consider the whole text.

How does Meg's mood change during the extract?

At the start, Meg is just watching the storm "wrapped in an old patchwork quilt". At the end, she "tossed the quilt down" because she has become angry and upset thinking about her bad day at school and her missing father.

Now try this

1. How does Meg's attitude to her bedroom change in the last few paragraphs?

71

Reading

Had a look ☐   Nearly there ☐   Nailed it! ☐

Authors' language

Effect

See page 54, Skill 3.

Authors can create different moods and feelings in their writing. You might be asked to find some words that the author has chosen to create a particular **effect**. Here's an example from *A Wrinkle in Time* (pages 64–65).

Question: Look at the first two paragraphs. Find and copy four words or phrases that suggest the storm is violent.

You will need to copy word-for word from the text. Choose the words or phrases you think make the best evidence.

> In her attic bedroom Margaret Murry, wrapped in an old patchwork quilt, sat on the foot of her bed and watched the <u>trees tossing</u> in the <u>frenzied lashing of the wind</u>. Behind the trees clouds scudded frantically across the sky. Every few moments the moon <u>ripped</u> through them, creating wraith-like shadows that raced along the ground.
> <u>The house shook.</u>

All these words and phrases suggest the storm is violent.

Answer: 1. trees tossing   2. frenzied lashing of the wind
3. ripped   4. the house shook

Meaning

See page 54, Skill 2.

You may be asked to explain what a particular word or phrase means and how it helps you understand the story and characters better.

Example

Why does the author use quote marks around "dumb baby brother"?

To show that some people (but not the narrator) think Charles Wallace is stupid but it's not what the author thinks.

Now try this

1. Find and copy three words or phrases that suggest the kitten is relaxed.

Had a look ☐   Nearly there ☐   Nailed it! ☐   **Reading**

Poem

Read this poem by Wes Magee.

At the End of the School Day

It is the end of a school day
    and down the long drive
come bag-swinging, shouting children.
    Deafened, the sky winces.
        The sun gapes in surprise.

Suddenly the runners skid to a stop,
    stand still and stare
at a small hedgehog
    curled-up on the tarmac
        like an old, frayed cricket ball.

A girl dumps her bag, tiptoes forward
    and gingerly, so gingerly
carries the creature
    to the safety of a shady hedge.
        Then steps back, watching.

Girl, children, sky and sun
    hold their breath.
There is a silence,
    a moment to remember
        on this warm afternoon in June.

Wes Magee

Reading poetry

Reading | Had a look ☐ | Nearly there ☐ | Nailed it! ☐

There are many different types of poem, but they all express feelings and ideas. Read a poem a few times and consider how the poet is using **form** and **imaginative language** to create meaning.

Form

The form of a poem means its rhythm, rhyme, repetitions, where lines start and end, and its shape. The form helps to give a poem its meaning. Here is an example from *At the End of a School Day* (page 73).

This line sits on its own to emphasise how the hedgehog is also on its own.

> Suddenly the runners skid to a stop,
> stand still and stare
> at a small hedgehog

The alliteration (st) gives the poem rhythm and an element of rhyme.

The lines ends with 'stare' to emphasise what everyone is doing.

Imaginative language

Poets also make feelings or ideas in poems more intense by using interesting vocabulary or figurative language.

'Bag-swinging' is an unusual adjective that suggests the children are rowdy.

> It is the end of a school day
> and down the long drive
> come bag-swinging, shouting children.
> Deafened, the sky winces.
> The sun gapes in surprise.

The personification of the sky and sun emphasises the children's bad behaviour.

Poetry questions test your ability to explain word choice and meaning.

Now try this

See page 54, Skills 2 and 3.

1. The poet writes "gingerly, so gingerly" in the third verse. What effect does this repetition have?
2. Why does everyone "hold their breath" in verse four?

See page 76 for more about noun personification.

Had a look ☐   Nearly there ☐   Nailed it! ☐   **Reading**

Similes and metaphors

Writers use **figurative language** to describe something in an interesting or imaginative way. This language can paint a picture in the reader's mind.

See page 54, Skill 3.

Similes

A **simile** is used to describe when two things are compared and said to be 'like' each other. The word 'as' is also used in similes.

…a small hedgehog curled-up like an old, frayed cricket ball.

The hedgehog isn't a cricket ball, but the simile helps describe what it looks like.

Declan felt as flat as a pancake after losing the football match.

Declan isn't a pancake, but the simile describes how low he feels.

Metaphors

Metaphors also compare two things. However, unlike similes, a metaphor states one thing is the other.

A book is a doorway to an adventure.

A book isn't a doorway, but this metaphor expresses how you might feel, as if you've entered an adventure when you read.

Example

Underline the simile in this sentence.

The grass under my feet was like a shaggy, green carpet.

The writer has used the word 'like' to compare the grass and the carpet, so it must be a simile.

Now try this

Are the sentences below using metaphors or similes?
1. Noel was as hungry as a horse after his long walk.
2. Mrs Fergus was like a bull in a china shop when she played badminton.
3. The sun was a glowing orange suspended above the horizon.
4. Shona is a walking encyclopedia.

Personification

Like similes and metaphors, **personification** is another form of figurative language.

> See page 54, Skills 3.

Non-human and human

A writer can make a non-human thing sound human by using personification and giving it human characteristics.

> Deafened, the sky <u>winces</u>.
> The sun <u>gapes</u> in surprise.

The sky can't wince, but the phrase suggests that the children's noise is painful.

The sun can't gape, but the phrase suggests the children's behaviour is a shock.

Using personification means the sky and sun are waiting along with the people to see what happens to the hedgehog.

> Girl, children, sky and sun <u>hold their breath</u>.

Example

Both of the verbs <u>gripped</u> and <u>stole</u> are usually actions a person does.

Underline the two pieces of personification in this sentence.

<u>Winter gripped the land</u> with its white fist and the bitter <u>wind stole my breath</u> away.

Now try this

Choose a suitable verb to complete each personification.

1. The floorboards _____ under the enormous weight of the giant.
2. The rain _____ against the windowpane.
3. The moon _____ from behind the silvery clouds.
4. The fire _____ the building in seconds.

Had a look ☐   Nearly there ☐   Nailed it! ☐   Reading

Alliteration and onomatopoeia

This type of figurative language is all about how words sound together or on their own to create an effect.

See page 54, Skill 3.

Alliteration

Alliteration is a series of words that all begin with the same sound. Writers often use alliteration in poetry, but it can be effective in story-writing too.

> Suddenly the runners skid to a stop, stand still and stare

If you say the poem out loud, saying st- makes you speak more slowly, like the children slowing down.

The letters **s** or **st** are repeated.

Onomatopoeia

Onomatopoeia is when the word copies the sound of the thing it is describing.

> The leaves rustled as the wind swooshed through the trees. Bang! The door slammed shut.

Each of these words sounds like what they are describing.

Example

*The word **gurgle** mimics the sound the water makes.*

Insert a suitable onomatopoeia into this sentence in the place shown.

The bath water *gurgled* merrily as it disappeared down the plug hole.

Now try this

Copy each sentence out, underlining the alliteration and circling the onomatopoeia.
1. The snake hissed and swayed silently from side to side.
2. The graceful goose glided towards the lake. The crack of a rifle filled the air.
3. At the farm show, the flags fluttered and the shivering, shaggy sheep baaed as they huddled together.

77

Answers

GRAMMAR

1 Nouns
1. happiness (abstract), rabbits (plural common), herd (collective), Ben (proper), Easter (proper), victory (common), deckchair (common)

2 Noun phrases
1. Answers may vary. Example: town – my town
2. Answers may vary. Examples: the <u>tall</u> girl, his <u>new</u> toy, some <u>crinkled</u> paper, your <u>enormous</u> fish, that <u>old</u> house.
3. Answers may vary. Example: <u>The small, unhappy boy</u> wandered into <u>the gloomy room full of cobwebs</u>.

3 Pronouns
1. <u>We</u>, <u>them</u>, <u>They</u>, <u>me</u>, <u>It</u>, <u>we</u>, <u>it</u>, <u>us</u>, <u>it</u>.

4 Possessive pronouns
1. Those books are <u>mine</u> although that magazine is <u>yours</u>.
2. Although <u>it's</u> nearly six o'clock, <u>it's</u> still not time for the cat to have <u>its</u> tea.

5 Determiners
1. <u>An</u> owl uses <u>its</u> face to gather sounds, just like <u>a</u> satellite dish collects signals for <u>your</u> television.

6 Adjectives
1. delicious, pink, sticky.
2. Aaron's mobile is <u>better</u> than mine, although Blake's is the <u>thinnest</u>.

7 Present tense
1. I <u>listen</u> to music every day; in fact, my radio <u>is playing</u> right now.
2. she <u>is running</u>, he <u>is studying</u> hard, we <u>are riding</u> our bikes, they <u>are being</u> rude
3. Answers may vary. Example: I wake up at 7.00 am.

8 Past tense
1. My parents <u>were talking</u> when someone <u>knocked</u> on the door. My dad <u>looked</u> puzzled. "I <u>wasn't expecting</u> anyone," he <u>said</u>.
2. it rained; they danced; you sulked; she hurried
3. While I spoke/ <u>was speaking</u> to George, the door suddenly <u>slammed</u>/ was slamming.

9 Perfect & future tenses
1. it <u>had</u> happened
2. Answers may vary. Example: I <u>am going to</u> leave for school after breakfast and I <u>will</u> return at four.

10 Tense consistency
1. Earlier this morning, Sammy went to the zoo, where he <u>saw</u> a mysterious animal. He should not have <u>gone</u> closer, but he couldn't resist. The animal, which <u>had</u> pink spots and blue toenails, <u>snarled</u> and snorted at him. The smell <u>was</u> terrible.

11 Modal verbs
1. could
2. Could; can't; can; must

12 Adverbs
1. Answers may vary. Example: "Let me out <u>now</u>," shouted Jack <u>crossly</u>.
2. Fortunately, hard, finally, Instead, beautifully

13 Adverbial phrases
1. <u>Once upon a time</u>, an old man lived <u>very happily</u> in a dark cave, where he made clothes <u>all by himself</u>.
2. Answers may vary. Example: <u>In complete terror</u>, Logan knocked on the ancient door of the old house.
3. Answers may vary. Example: The concert hall was crowded, we couldn't sit anywhere near the front.

Answers

14 Conjunctions
1. Answers may vary. Example: <u>Although</u> it was snowing, Howard <u>and</u> Tamwar played football <u>until</u> they lost their ball.

15 Prepositions
1. Katy walked <u>for</u> two hours <u>through</u> the dark tunnel. Finally, she saw a light coming <u>towards</u> her.

16 Statements and questions
1. Mason is fit enough to play in the match today.
2. Are Katrina and Scott the winners of the science competition?

17 Commands and exclamations
1. Go up to your room! (command), What a lovely day it is! (exclamation), Push the buzzer and enter. (command), How shocking that was! (exclamation).

18 Subject and object
1. Candace was singing <u>a song</u>. (object)
   The cat swallowed <u>it</u>. (object)
   <u>The desperate prisoner</u> disappeared into the forest. (subject)
   <u>We</u> were dancing, weren't we? (subject)

19 Active and passive
1. Passive. The tigers are having the protection 'done to' them by law.
2. The thief tripped the alarm. The security guard alerted the police but, before they arrived, two passers-by grabbed the thief.

20 Phrases
1. Expanded noun phrase

21 Main clauses
1. Shani's pony doesn't like carrots <u>nor</u> will it eat parsnips.
2. Following his accident, <u>Jarrod spent two days in hospital</u> but, against the advice of his doctor, <u>he went home early</u>.

22 Subordinate clauses
1. <u>Unless</u> it was a special occasion, my grandparents always went to bed early <u>because</u> they were getting old.
2. Before you have your tea, you must bring your toys inside.

23 Relative clauses
1. The ice-creams, <u>which</u> had been sitting in the sunshine, had melted.
2. My grandad, <u>who is 72,</u> is running the marathon.

24 Subject verb agreement
1. Bertie <u>sings</u> really well.
   Kayley and Jared <u>brush</u> the kitchen floor.
2. The <u>pilots</u> fly their planes.
   The <u>train</u> is late.
   The <u>kettles</u> have boiled.

25 Standard English
1. My dad wants to go to the cinema but I don't want to go.
   We haven't done anything wrong.

PUNCTUATION

26 Capital letters
1. <u>I</u>t's time <u>I</u> went to <u>B</u>irmingham.
   <u>K</u>athy borrowed that money last <u>M</u>arch. Now it's nearly <u>N</u>ovember!
   The <u>S</u>t <u>L</u>uke's <u>C</u>hurch <u>C</u>hoir sang carols in <u>I</u>talian and <u>G</u>erman at <u>C</u>hristmas.

79

Answers

27 Ending a sentence

1. Was it time to go home? The chef looked at his watch. It was eleven o'clock. He smiled. Finally, his shift was over. What a day!

28 Commas in lists

1. Would you like strawberries, yoghurt or a piece of watermelon?
2. Mohan had three books, two pens, a hat and a sandwich in his bag.
3. Answers may vary. Examples: ladies and gentlemen, bread and butter, lamb and mint, life or death, fun and games, flesh and blood, lock and key, pots and pans

29 Commas for clarity

1. Before dawn, Leila, whose kitten was sick, took it straight to the vets.
2. Some kangaroos, which can grow up to two metres tall, are extremely strong.

30 Parenthesis

1. The children were scared and miserable – the electricity had gone off – when the storm hit.
2. Yasmin Blythe, from near Bolton, won first prize in the competition.

31 Colons

1. For his birthday this is what Dexter wanted: roller skates, a kite, a trampoline and a cricket bat.
2. I have lots of hobbies: art, netball, reading and dancing.
   After the second heat it was clear: Johan was unbeatable.

32 Semi-colons

1. The rain poured down; the rising river soon burst its banks.
2. I don't like any of these types of weather: cold, frosty mornings; sticky, humid nights; never-ending drizzle; or baking-hot afternoons in the classroom.

33 Apostrophes : possession

1. Agnes' mobile (incorrect: Agnes's mobile), the men's changing room (correct), Harrys' duck (incorrect: Harry's duck), the wolves' territory (correct), the women's successes (correct), the foxe's den (incorrect: the foxes' den)

34 Apostrophes : contraction

1. They'll be home soon, who's going shopping?, it's time for tea, we're hungry
2. I would like to go swimming, but it will be too cold and I will not enjoy it.

35 Punctuating speech

1. "How old are you tomorrow?" asked Perry.
   Chris replied, "Eleven. When's your birthday?"
   "Not until July!" groaned Perry. "I can't wait."

36 Hyphens and single dashes

1. Students own answer. Example: Without a hyphen 'Man eating lion' suggests that a man is eating a lion. Man-eating lion spotted lurking in woodland.
2. You should send a present to your Granny – just make sure you post it before Tuesday.

SPELLING

37 Word families

1. see
2. construction, destruct, infrastructure
3. Answers may vary. Examples: dismiss, mission, missile, intermission, transmission, admission

38 Prefixes

1. antisocial, imperfect, bicycle, prehistoric
2. illegal, deactivate, unhelpful, dishonest

39 Suffixes

1. Answers may vary. Example: colourful, awesome, magical, foolish, poisonous, daily

Answers

40 Synonyms and antonyms
1. dismal/bleak, mocking/sarcastic
2. Answers may vary. Example: The <u>hilarious</u> play was full of <u>interesting</u> characters and <u>breath-taking</u> scenes.

41 Plurals
1. We bought two avocado**s**, some strawberr**ies** and three lo**aves** of bread.
   Pupp**ies**, kangaroo**s** and fish**es** are my favourite animal**s**.

42 Tricky spellings
1. lib<u>r</u>ary, <u>r</u>hyme, av<u>e</u>rage, han<u>d</u>kerchief, enviro<u>n</u>ment, mus<u>c</u>le, def<u>i</u>nitely

43 More tricky spellings
1. rough, enough
2. seized, achieve, Neither, believe

44 Homophones
1. mourning, passed, led

WRITING

45 Audience and purpose
1. Example genres:

   Fiction: fairy tales, adventure, science fiction, poems, myths, legends, play scripts, fables, comedies, detective stories, fantasy, horror, mysteries, satires, thrillers, short stories

   Non-fiction: reports, articles, explanations, biographies, autobiographies, adverts, persuasive writing, recounts, glossaries, indexes, essays, dictionaries, encyclopaedias

47 Writing and editing
1. Answers may vary. Example: <u>Enraged</u>, the bull <u>charged at</u> the <u>frightened</u> walkers<u>, who clambered back over the fence</u>.

48 Checking
1. During Queen Victoria's reign, young lads called mudlarks waded at low tide in the filthy mud of the River Thames where they searched for scraps of led, iron and other waste to sell.

51 Writing persuasive letters
1. Answers may vary. Example: they don't live in a suitable area, the school field is perfect for astronomy, the fence will keep them safe, they will give Ms Mellor a photo, they will write good things about the school, they will name a planet after Ms Mellor.

52 Writing balanced arguments
1. Answers may vary. Example:

   For: children might not be listening properly when someone tells them something important.

   Against: restricting 'screen time' might mean children can't do their homework properly.

READING

56 Question types: selected answers
1. fact ✓, opinion ✓, fact ✓

61 Retrieving and recording
1. (every) March
2. as gourmet food

62 Point, Evidence, Explain (PEE)
1. Answers may vary. Example: The fine-mesh fence solution is the most cruel. We know the toads "die in large numbers" because "the fences hold them back". We know that they can only survive if they have "constant access to moisture" and that they "are attracted to the water". This shows that the toads, who are only using their natural instincts, are drawn to their own deaths on purpose.

Answers

66 Character
1. Answers may vary. Example: I think Meg is an unhappy person. She wishes she could hide her feelings and she loses her temper easily. She is protective of her baby brother.

67 Theme
1. Answers may vary. Example: I think the theme will be the relationship between Meg and Charles Wallace and how they find their missing father. I think things will get better for Meg.

68 Finding meaning
1. wrongdoer

69 Inference
1. Answers may vary. Example: She is furious and feeling protective because she attacks a boy who insults her brother and ends up in a fight.
2. Answers may vary. Example: She feels upset because he has disappeared and she doesn't know where he is or when he might come back. She is also hurt because people are gossiping about why he's gone.

70 Predicting
1. Answers may vary. Example: I predict the boy she fought with might try to get his own back by spreading more 'vicious rumours' about her dad. I think Meg might cry and the girls might laugh at her for acting like a baby again.

71 Making comparisons
1. Answers may vary. Example: When she asked to have the attic bedroom, she thought it was a 'privilege' because she was 'the oldest'. During the storm, she now feels like it's a 'punishment'.

72 Authors' language
1. yawned, went back to sleep, stretched luxuriously

74 Reading poetry
1. Answers may vary. Example: This emphasises how carefully the girl is carrying the hedgehog.
2. Answers may vary. Example: They are waiting to see if the hedgehog is going to recover or not.

75 Similes and metaphors
1. simile
2. simile
3. metaphor
4. metaphor

76 Personification
1. Answers may vary. Examples: groaned, complained
2. Answers may vary. Examples: hammered, slammed
3. Answers may vary. Examples: peaked out, sailed out
4. Answers may vary. Examples: consumed, devoured

77 Alliteration and onomatopoeia
1. The snake (hissed) and swayed silently from side to side.
2. The graceful goose glided towards the lake. The (crack) of a rifle filled the air.
3. At the farm show, the flags fluttered and the shivering, shaggy sheep (baaed) as they huddled together.

Published by Pearson Education Limited, 80 Strand, London, WC2R 0RL.

www.pearsonschools.co.uk

Text © Pearson Education Limited 2016
Edited by Jane Cotter
Typeset by Jouve India Private Limited
Produced by Elektra Media
Original illustrations © Pearson Education Limited 2016
Illustrated by Elektra Media
Cover illustration by Ana Albero

The right of Giles Clare to be identified as author of this work has been asserted by him in accordance with the Copyright, Designs and Patents Act 1988.

First published 2016

British Library Cataloguing in Publication Data
A catalogue record for this book is available from the British Library.

ISBN 978 1 292 14601 0

Copyright notice
All rights reserved. No part of this publication may be reproduced in any form or by any means (including photocopying or storing it in any medium by electronic means and whether or not transiently or incidentally to some other use of this publication) without the written permission of the copyright owner, except in accordance with the provisions of the Copyright, Designs and Patents Act 1988 or under the terms of a licence issued by the Copyright Licensing Agency, Saffron House, 6–10 Kirby Street, London EC1N 8TS (www.cla.co.uk). Applications for the copyright owner's written permission should be addressed to the publisher.

Acknowledgements
We are grateful to the following for permission to reproduce copyright material:

Text
Poetry on page 73 from *The Works*, Pan Macmillan (W. Magee 2010), reproduced by permission of the author, Wes Magee; Extract on page 64 from *A Wrinkle in Time* Puffin Classics (M. L'Engle 1963), For Worldwide except for U.S used by permission of the author, Madeleine L'Engle; Extract on page 64 from *A Wrinkle in Time* Puffin Classics (M. L'Engle 1963). For the US/Canadian rights, *A Wrinkle in Time* © 1962 by Madeleine L'Engle. Reprinted by permission of Farar, Straus, and Giroux, LLC.
All rights reserved

Picture credits
The publisher would like to thank the following for their kind permission to reproduce their photographs:

(Key: b-bottom; c-centre; l-left; r-right; t-top)

Shutterstock.com: Johan Larson 58b, laine 59, Yukikae4B 58t

All other images © Pearson Education